Myth, Philosophy, and Literature

Olivier Serrat

Myth, Philosophy, and Literature

Exploring Thought, Story, and Culture

 Springer

Olivier Serrat (ID)
School of Continuing Studies
Georgetown University
Washington, DC, USA

ISBN 978-981-95-2896-7   ISBN 978-981-95-2897-4   (eBook)
https://doi.org/10.1007/978-981-95-2897-4

This Springer imprint is published by the registered company Springer Nature Singapore Pte Ltd.
The registered company address is: 152 Beach Road, #21-01/04 Gateway East, Singapore 189721, Singapore

If disposing of this product, please recycle the paper.

Preface

Where do we come from? What are we? Where are we going? In an oil painting from 1897 to 1898, Paul Gauguin (1848–1903)—a trailblazing French Post-Impressionist celebrated for revolutionizing artistic conventions through Symbolism—employs a triptych format to explore these questions. The composition, which measures 139 × 375 cm (approximately 54.7 × 147.6 in), was intended to be viewed from right to left. On the right, a small group of women with a sleeping infant symbolizes the beginning of life; the central section captures the immediacy of everyday moments; and the leftmost section depicts a huddled older woman, hinting at the approach of death. In the upper left corner of the canvas, Gauguin inscribed the three conundrums in French—*D'où Venons Nous/ Que Sommes Nous/ Où Allons Nous*—omitting punctuation to lend the text a timeless quality. Regarded as a seminal work by art historians and critics, Gauguin's magnum opus stands as the culmination of his artistic journey, conveying both the beauty and tragedy of his South Pacific experiences. Gauguin's fusion of word and image does not offer conclusions but encourages meditation.

Similarly, myth, philosophy, and literature have woven themselves into the rich fabric of our culture. Myth preserves our ancestral narratives and primeval roots. Philosophy dares us to confront the nature of reality and morality. Literature enshrines the complexities of love, loss, triumph, and defeat—both in factual and fictional realms [Serrat, O. (2022). *Flash fiction: 22 very short stories.* Troubador Publishing Ltd.; Serrat, O. (2023). *Mere words, these: 32 poems in free verse.* Troubador Publishing Ltd.]. Like Gauguin's threefold arrangement, myth, philosophy, and literature embody facets of our shared inquiry, binding the particular to the universal.

Myth, Philosophy, and Literature: Exploring Thought, Story, and Culture brings these distinct voices into a unified vision. This book invites you to travel through time, uncovering the hidden connections among myth, philosophy, and literature. Each chapter—resonating with Gauguin's questions—stands on its own, with topics listed in alphabetical order in the table of contents for easy exploration.

The book is organized into three parts. The first section, *Dawn of the Western Tradition*, examines foundational ideas from ancient Mesopotamia and the Mediterranean (circa 2000 BCE), situating them within the historical development of modern Western thought. By melding time-honored insights with current contemplations, this section reinvigorates the conversation between our past and our present. The second section, *Epistemologies of Knowledge*, offers a comparative analysis of diverse, cross-cultural perspectives on knowledge. Drawing upon Western, Daoist, and Buddhist sources, this discussion offers new insight into the age-old debate between religion and science, while exploring alternative epistemological frameworks—including African *ubuntu*, Indigenous storytelling, Islamic intellectual traditions, and Indian philosophies. This section challenges readers to think about how ancient wisdom continues to shape deliberations and individual convictions alike. The third section, *Literary Phenomenology and Cultural Contexts: Exploring Identity, Truth, and Ecology*, addresses essential issues concerning the construction of meaning, the interpretation of reality, and the formation of intellectual traditions. Spanning pre-modern, modern, and postmodern contexts, this part reveals the dynamic between our personal narratives and our collective experiences, prompting readers to reconsider the constructs that shape our identities in a dynamic world.

Taken as a whole, this book seeks to clarify Gauguin's enigmas of origin, essence, and destiny by bridging historical perspectives with modern concerns. As you turn each page, let yourself be stirred by the richness of humankind's collective past. You may find echoes of your own journey. Take time to reflect on your beliefs and personal experiences as you explore these themes and their meaning for our shared humanity.

Dedication Pierre Serrat (1931–2014) embodied an uncommon pairing: a civil engineer by trade and a wayfarer at heart [Serrat, O. (2021). Life-markers and personal values. In: *Leading solutions: Essays in business psychology* (pp. 55–56). Springer]. Practical minds and desire find their richest expression when they work in harmony. In the same way, myth, philosophy, and literature—at their best—reveal the many shades of our inner and shared lives when they mingle. On these themes, he would surely have appreciated the following reflections:

Myth is an attempt to narrate a whole human experience, of which the purpose is too deep, going too deep in the blood and soul, for mental explanation or description

—D. H. Lawrence

Miracles are so called because they excite wonder. In unphilosophical minds any rare or unexpected thing excites wonder, while in philosophical minds the familiar excites wonder also

—George Santayana

That is part of the beauty of all literature. You discover that your longings are universal longings, that you're not lonely and isolated from anyone. You belong

—F. Scott Fitzgerald

Washington, DC, USA   Olivier Serrat

Acknowledgment I extend my deepest gratitude to Anushangi Weerakoon, Senior Editor at Springer Singapore, whose dedication made this book possible. Our collaboration began when William Achauer, Editorial Director at Springer Singapore, introduced us after the publication of *Knowledge Solutions: Tools, Methods, and Approaches to Drive Organizational Performance* (2017). Anushangi oversaw the production of *Leading Solutions: Essays in Business Psychology* (2021), and just two years later, I pitched *Digital Solutions: Reframing Leadership* (2023). At the time, she exclaimed, "I did not think I would work with you so soon!" I trust she has not regretted that remark—because little did she know, it was only the beginning. That same year, we embarked on our next project: *Leading Organizations of the Future: A New Framework* (2023), followed by *Anthropogenic Solutions for Climate Change: Achieving Environmental Peace* (2025). This marks our fifth collaboration in four years—a true testament to our shared pursuit of excellence. Will there be another? No. Absolutely not. "Good is knowing when to stop," wrote Toni Morrison. We are done. *Finis.* (Anushangi, stop reading here.) Well … perhaps one more.

Washington, DC, USA   Olivier Serrat

Competing Interests The author has no competing interests to declare that are relevant to the content of this manuscript.

Contents

List of Figures

Part I

Dawn of the Western Tradition

1

Gilgamesh: An Epic for All Seasons

1.1 The Cradle of Civilization

The seeds of the world's earliest civilization were sown at the close of the Paleolithic era, ca. 10,000 BCE, when our ancestors first settled in Mesopotamia (from Ancient Greek Μεσοποταμία "[land] between rivers"). In a vast desert, regular flooding by the Tigris and the Euphrates deposited silt and made the soil fertile. People began to domesticate plants (e.g., barley, beans, lentils, peas, wheat) and animals (e.g., cattle, chicken, goats, pig, sheep) to fulfill their needs. Then, beginning about 6000 BCE, irrigation infrastructure (viz., canals, channels, aqueducts) was built to bring fresh water to fields. The birth of agriculture was a pivotal moment in history: sedentary communities were able to produce food more efficiently, which released labor for other purposes and, in turn, increased creativity, innovation, and productivity from specialization. Centers of population emerged, calling for new acts and processes of governing. From ca. 4500 BCE, urbanization spread across the region with a group of city-states such as Eridu, Kish, Lagash, Nippur, Umma, Ur, and the world's first true city, Uruk (today known as Warka, in Iraq). A hub of trade and administration, Uruk may in its late phase ca. 3100 BCE have had about 40,000 inhabitants and up to 90,000 people living in its environs. Uruk is celebrated as the birthplace of writing ca. 3200 BCE. Besides writing, the inventions of the Mesopotamian people, viz., Sumerians and Akkadians but also Babylonians and Assyrians, included accounting, monumental architecture (i.e., the ziggurat), beer, cartography,

O. Serrat, *Myth, Philosophy, and Literature*,
https://doi.org/10.1007/978-981-95-2897-4_1

codified laws, mass-produced bricks and pottery, mathematics, sails, cylinder seals and envelopes, the concept of time, and the wheel. In turn, the Sumerians, Akkadians, Babylonians, and Assyrians dominated Mesopotamia from ca. 3100 BCE to the fall of Babylon in 539 BCE when the region was conquered by Cyrus the Great (ca. 600–530 BCE), the founder of the Achaemenid Empire (i.e., the First Persian Empire).

1.2   *The Epic,* Starring Gilgamesh

The English word *epic* entered the language via the French word *épique* or directly from Latin *epicus* which itself derives from the Ancient Greek adjective ἐπικός (*epikos*), from ἔπος (*epos*), which simply means "a word; a tale, story; promise, prophecy, proverb; poetry in heroic verse" (Etymonline, 2025). In literature, an epic is "a long, often book-length, narrative in verse form that retells the heroic journey of a single person, or group of persons" (Poets.org. 2023, para. 1). In common parlance, the word *epic*also refers to something that extends beyond the usual or ordinary, notably in scope.

Rooted in oral traditions, epic poetry is humanity's oldest literary genre: its oldest surviving written expression is *The Epic of Gilgamesh* (George, 2003). Composed in the Akkadian language ca. 2100–1200 BCE, *The Epic of Gilgamesh* is a poem of about 2000 lines, painstakingly inscribed on 11 clay tablets in cuneiform script with a sharpened reed stylus. A logo-syllabic script, cuneiform was used in Mesopotamia to write several languages of the ancient Near East. *The Epic of Gilgamesh* was discovered in 1853, when a 12-tablet version was found in the ruins of the library of Ashurbanipal (ca. 685–631 BCE) in Nineveh. Originally, *The Epic of Gilgamesh* may have been 3000 lines-long.

The Epic of Gilgamesh purports to proclaim to the world the deeds of the eponymous sovereign of Uruk. (Most historians agree that Gilgamesh was a historical king who ruled Uruk ca. 2600 BCE.) At the start, Gilgamesh is lustful and tyrannical, an unstable compound that is two parts god and one part man. To stop Gilgamesh from oppressing the people of Uruk, the gods create a wild man called Enkidu. But Gilgamesh and Enkidu are equally matched, become inseparable friends, and embark on adventures. In the Cedar Forest they kill Humbaba the Terrible and cut the trees: this angers the gods because they had tasked Humbaba with guarding the forest. Then, Gilgamesh rejects Ishtar, the goddess of love and war. Ishtar calls on her father Nanna, the moon god, to send the Bull of Heaven and punish Gilgamesh; however, Gilgamesh and Enkidu manage to slay the beast. And so, the gods decide that Enkidu must die: his health deteriorates over the course of 12 days and he finally meets his doom after being made to see the underworld in a dream. Gilgamesh is distraught and, having come to fear death, sets off to discover the secret of eternal life. Gilgamesh is ferried across the waters of death and finds Utnapishtim, who survived the Great Flood by heeding the gods and building an ark in preparation. Utnapishtim advises Gilgamesh to dive into the ocean to find a plant that makes whoever possesses it young again. Gilgamesh brings the plant to the surface but it is stolen and eaten by a snake; for this reason, Gilgamesh will be equal in death with others. At long last, Gilgamesh returns to Uruk and marvels at the grandeur of his city: "It's not how you start; it's how you finish," one imagines him saying. Summarizing, *The Epic of Gilgamesh* has a headstrong ruler face reality after his friend dies: ultimately, Gilgamesh realizes that immortality is—if anything—the legacy one leaves behind.

1.3 Epic Poetry and Heroic Themes After Gilgamesh

In its time and thereafter, *The Epic of Gilgamesh* must have been widely known. Remarkably, a few episodes in *The Epic of Gilgamesh* foreshadow later stories in Biblical literature (e.g., the Fall of Man, when Enkidu's harmony with nature is broken by Shamhat, who initiates him to knowledge of good and evil; the fruits of the Tree of Life, as when the magic plant is stolen by a serpent; the Great Flood; verses in the Book of Ecclesiastes). *The Epic of Gilgamesh* also laid the foundations of the tradition of heroic sagas and evidently influenced subsequent classic works such as *The Iliad* and *The Odyssey* by Homer who—give or take a century or two—is believed to have flourished about 1500 years later ca. 750 BCE. In the wake of *The Epic of Gilgamesh*, Fig. 1.1 showcases a dozen great epic poems.

The Epic of Gilgamesh defined the foremost heroic themes:

- *Superhuman Characteristics.* The hero has special powers (and enjoys the help of a god or goddess). The hero is bolder, braver, stronger, and cleverer than others. The hero often has a divine parent but human heritage implies mortality.
- *A Matchless Ego.* The hero seeks fame, glory, and honor: to the hero, these are of greater consequence than life itself.
- *A Far Traveler.* The hero is on a quest, sometimes with companions, facing challenges no mere mortal could possibly surmount.

ca. 22nd Century BCE	• *The Epic of Gilgamesh*—Anonymous
8th Century BCE	• *The Iliad* and *The Odyssey*—Homer
8thCentury BCE—3rd Century AD	• *Ramayana*—Maharishi Valmiki (Attributed)
3rdCentury BCE	• *The Argonautica*—Apollonius of Rhodes
3rdCentury BCE—3rdCentury AD	• *Mahabharata*—Vyāsa (Attributed)
1stCentury BCE	• *The Aeneid*—Virgil
700s	• *Beowulf*—Anonymous
1300s	• *The Divine Comedy*—Dante
1500s	• *The Faerie Queen*—Spenser
1600s	• *Paradise Lost*—Milton
1800s	• *Don Juan*—Byron

Fig. 1.1 A selection of epic poetry through the ages. *Note* From Serrat (2023)

• *A Flaw.* The hero has a shortcoming (e.g., excessive pride, a raging temper).

Aeneas, Aragorn, Arjuna, (King) Arthur, Beowulf, Gatsby, Grettir, Hamlet, Hercules, Macbeth, Odysseus, Oedipus, Othello, Roland, Romeo, Rostam (or Rustam), Siegfried … These characters were cast in the same tragic mold as Gilgamesh but Achilles comes closest. The bravest, finest, and greatest warrior in *The Iliad*, Achilles is proud, impulsive, and holds grudges: when provoked, he flies berserker-like into a rage. After he has killed Hektor, Achilles remains so consumed by the death of Patroklos that he lets Achaean soldiers stab and mutilate Hektor's corpse; next, he ties the body to his chariot and drags it 12 times around Patroklos' funeral pyre. Figure 1.2 compares the characters and circumstances of Achilles and Gilgamesh: the similarities suggest that the former's personality could have been patterned after the latter's.

Odysseus also shares several of the defining character traits of epic heroes. Unlike Achilles, he may not have superhuman characteristics; but, he has a matchless ego, he is a far traveler, and he has a flaw. Odysseus comes equipped with confidence, courage, nobility, strength, a thirst for glory, and the sharpest of intellects; that last character trait feeds hubris, the fatal flaw that leads to his suffering and the death of all his companions.

Much as the other epic heroes who followed, such as Achilles and Odysseus, Gilgamesh performs extraordinary feats. Yet, Gilgamesh is

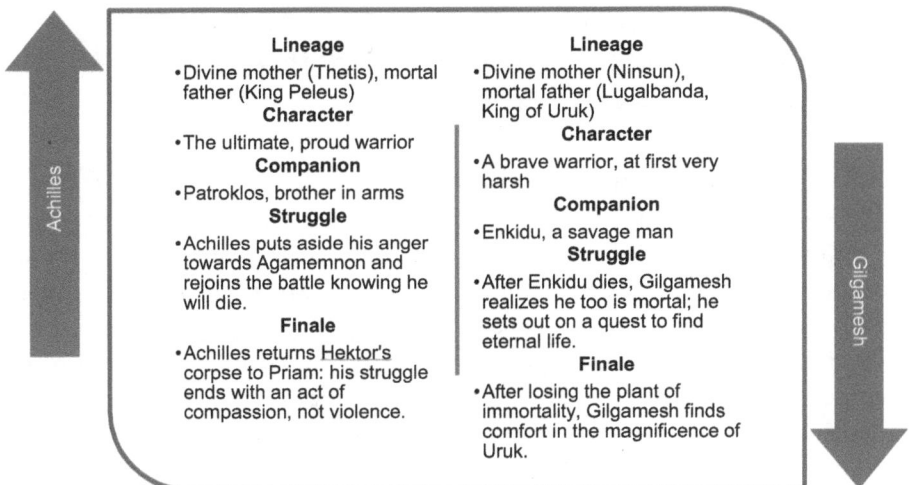

Fig. 1.2 Achilles meets Gilgamesh. *Note* From Serrat (2023)

a hero with a difference: atypically, he does not follow a code of honor or protect his people. Quite the reverse, Gilgamesh lacks moral purpose, abuses his subjects, is driven by fear of death, and does not achieve his quest. What, then, are we to make of *The Epic of Gilgamesh*? Becker (1973) comes to mind. In Becker (1973), the "vital lie" has to do with how human beings formulate heroic strategies to pass over their mortality. Becker (1973) accepted that the denial of death was a necessary component of functioning in the world but contended that it obscures genuine self-knowledge. Becker's (1973) insight is relevant to *The Epic of Gilgamesh*, mortality being its central theme. In a related manner, Leeming (2022) saw heroic acts as metaphors for the human condition: a hero rejects mortality and struggles against monsters in search of identity.

The last words in *The Epic of Gilgamesh* summon the listener (or reader) to walk along the walls of Uruk, take in its vast splendors, and see how excellently all is constructed. Conversely, therefore, it is because Gilgamesh is so flawed at the outset that we celebrate his titanic travails, commiserate when he loses the plant of rejuvenation in his grasp, and commend his tardy existential realization that the most meaningful life you can have is to be your best. Superhuman characteristics, a matchless ego, a far traveler, a flaw . . . By highlighting these foremost heroic themes, narrative works of poetry mean to teach us valuable moral lessons from such as Gilgamesh, Achilles, and Odysseus so we might apply them to our lives.

1.4   Compare and Contrast: *The Epic of Gilgamesh, the Iliad,* and *the Odyssey* Meet Booker (2004)

The foregoing pointed out the influence of the heroic themes in *The Epic of Gilgamesh*, notably with respect to the characters of Achilles and Odysseus in *The Iliad* and *The Odyssey* by Homer. But, there is more to be surprised about if one also examines *The Epic of Gilgamesh*, *The Iliad*, and *The Odyssey* from the perspective of their plots.

Inspired by Jung's (1947) model of the psyche (i.e., the ego, the personal unconscious, the collective unconscious), specifically the proposition that underneath the superficial levels of the individual psyche we all share the same psychological make-up, Booker (2004) researched whether there might be basic plots (or themes) to the stories in our world. It is worth noting that, similarly influenced by Jung (1947), Campbell (1949) had previously identified a structure, i.e., stages or steps, in the journeys of archetypal heroes. Using ancient myths and folk takes, the plays and novels of great literature, and popular movies or television shows, Booker (2004) demonstrated that seven archetypal themes recur in every kind of storytelling: (a) overcoming the monster, (b) rags to riches, (c) the quest, (d) voyage and return, (e) comedy, (f) tragedy, and (g) rebirth. Booker (2004) mentioned two other basic plots that were not included in the list of archetypal themes because they do not have extensive stages: (a) rebellion against "the one" (e.g., *Nineteen Eighty-Four*), and (b) the mystery (e.g., *The Murders in the Rue Morgue*). Booker (2004) also submitted that five meta-plots underpin fiction works irrespective of their basic themes: (a) anticipation, (b) dream, (c) frustration, (d) nightmare, and (e) resolution. (Put straightforwardly, the five meta-plots represent the three stages of a story that sets in motion, develops, and concludes.) Figure 1.3 sums up Booker's (2004) seven basic plots.

For illustrative purposes, Fig. 1.4 fits nine works to each of Booker's (2004) seven basic plots.

Referencing Booker (2004), it looks as if *The Epic of Gilgamesh* combines not less than four of the seven basic plots: (a) overcoming the monster, (b) the quest, (c) voyage and return, and (d) rebirth, even if it is fundamentally a quest. The multiplicity of themes in *The Epic of Gilgamesh* explains the richness of its storyline:

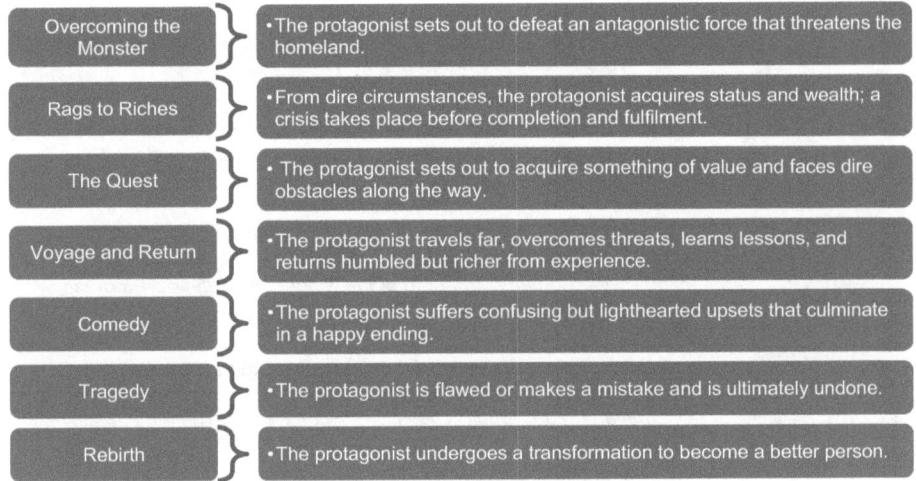

Overcoming the Monster	• The protagonist sets out to defeat an antagonistic force that threatens the homeland.
Rags to Riches	• From dire circumstances, the protagonist acquires status and wealth; a crisis takes place before completion and fulfilment.
The Quest	• The protagonist sets out to acquire something of value and faces dire obstacles along the way.
Voyage and Return	• The protagonist travels far, overcomes threats, learns lessons, and returns humbled but richer from experience.
Comedy	• The protagonist suffers confusing but lighthearted upsets that culminate in a happy ending.
Tragedy	• The protagonist is flawed or makes a mistake and is ultimately undone.
Rebirth	• The protagonist undergoes a transformation to become a better person.

Fig. 1.3 Archetypal themes in Booker (2004). *Note* From Serrat (2023)

- *Overcoming the Monster.* Gilgamesh faces threats from monsters (i.e., Humbaba, the Bull of Heaven) that he must overcome with courage and skill.
- *The Quest.* Gilgamesh's journey is driven by his desire to find immortality and escape death, a motif in many quest stories.
- *Voyage and Return.* Gilgamesh's voyage takes him across land, sea, and the bottom of the ocean where he encounters strange creatures and beholds wondrous or terrifying sights (e.g., the Cedar Forest, the Garden of the Gods, the Gate of the Scorpion Men, Siduri's Tavern, the Waters of Death) before he returns to Uruk.
- *Rebirth.* Gilgamesh's rebirth occurs when he realizes that he cannot escape his fate but can still live a meaningful life by ruling well and bequeathing a legacy.

What of *The Iliad*? Strangely, Booker (2004) did not characterize *The Iliad*, which is not even mentioned in the bibliography, index of stories cited, or the general index of that book. Exactingly, Booker (2004) contended that a quest unfolds via certain steps: (a) the call, (b) the journey, (c) arrival and frustration, (d) the final ordeals, and (e) the goal. What with multiple characters and subplots, not all elements of *The Iliad* fit perfectly in Booker's (2004) structure for quests: might this explain Booker's (2004) disregard? Nevertheless, *The Iliad* probably qualifies as a quest because it involves a long campaign against Troy:

Fig. 1.4 Fitting works to plot types. *Note* From Serrat (2023)

- *The Call.* The conflict between the Achaeans and Troy is ignited when Paris, a son of Priam, seizes Helen from Menelaus. The Achaeans set sail toward Troy to win Helen back. The Trojan War is the call.
- *The Journey.* The journey is the Trojan War per se, with its many battles, challenges, and recurring turns of events. The journey takes a turn for the worse when Agamemnon and Achilles argue over Briseis: Achilles refuses to render further service in the Achaean army and the Achaeans flounder in the absence of their best warrior.
- *Arrival and Frustration.* At length, the prospects of the Achaeans improve when nighttime scouting by Diomedes and Odysseus yields information about Troy's plans. Despite this, the following day brings disaster when the Trojans break through the defenses of the Achaeans.
- *The Final Ordeals.* Wearing Achilles' armor, Patroklos is slain by Hektor. Achilles mourns beside Patroklos' body: he beats the ground and cries loudly.

- *The Goal.* Achilles is filled with such grief and rage that he rejoins the battle, which marks the final turning point in the Trojan War.

On the other hand, Booker (2004) deemed *The Odyssey* the quintessential quest and adjudged that "[...] there is no more complete and profound version [...]" (p. 250). Even so, I detected in *The Odyssey* significant elements of voyage and—especially—return as well as rebirth illustrated by:

- *Voyage and Return.* Odysseus faces repeated singular challenges on his journey to Ithaca. To wit, Odysseus and his companions land in Ismaros where they enslave men: this angers Zeus, who sends a storm that forces Odysseus and his men to dock on Djerba then Sicily. Odysseus encounters Polyphemus, a cyclops, and blinds him: this incenses Poseidon because Polyphemus is his son. Odysseus and his companions arrive in the Land of the Lotus Eaters. Odysseus has a love affair with Circe, a witch-goddess. Odysseus and his men are tempted by deadly sirens. Odysseus journeys into Hades to consult Teiresias, a prophet, and gain knowledge of how he might return to Ithaca. Odysseus prevails over Scylla, a sea monster. All of Odysseus' companions die before he finally reaches home, alone, and fights off Penelope's suitors in a climactic scene.
- *Rebirth.* Odysseus is known for his sharp intellect but the 10-year struggle to reach Ithaca transforms him: he becomes a humbler man; he learns patience and thinks harder before he acts; he communicates better with his men; he stops longing for glory and simply wants to return home. From this optic, *The Odyssey* is as much about personal growth and triumph over adversity as it is about quest.

Of course, as in the case of *The Epic of Gilgamesh* and *The Odyssey*, some stories can incorporate elements taken from more than one of the seven basic plots. Besides, each of the seven basic plots can have different versions (e.g., artistic style, dark or light conclusions, degree of realism).

1.5   Gilgamesh: First Existential Hero and Timeless Quester

Paul Gauguin's 1897 oil masterpiece flags three questions, inscribed on the top left corner of the canvas: "D'où venons-nous? Que sommes-nous? Où allons-nous?" ("Where do we come from? What are we? Where are we going?") No one knows who composed *The Epic of Gilgamesh* nearly 4000 years ago, nor for what audience, but it is a surprisingly humanistic work that deals with these central questions about human existence. *The Epic of Gilgamesh* prototyped the heroic saga and made possible numerous classic works. *The Epic of Gilgamesh*, *The Iliad*, and *The Odyssey* are all quests: their protagonists set out to acquire something of value and face dire obstacles along the way. Of course, *The Epic of Gilgamesh* is the more primitive of the three and seemingly imparts a pessimistic view of life; *The Iliad* is the most true-to-life and tragic; and *The Odyssey* is the most sophisticated and, ultimately, optimistic. Be that as it may, all three are versions of a basic story, viz., the quest, that has endured through time.

References

Becker E (1973) The denial of death. The Free Press

Booker C (2004) The seven basic plots: why we tell stories. Bloomsbury

Campbell J (1949) The hero with a thousand faces. Pantheon Books

Etymonline (2025). Epic. In www.etymonline.com. https://www.etymonline.com/word/epic

George A (2003) The epic of Gilgamesh (trans: George A). Penguin Classics

Jung C (1947) On the nature of the psyche. Ark Paperbacks

Leeming D (2022) World mythology: a very short introduction. Oxford University Press

Poets.org. (2023). Epic. In www.poets.org. https://poets.org/glossary/epic

Serrat O (2023) Gilgamesh: the prototypical epic hero. [PowerPoint slides]. Georgetown University. https://www.researchgate.net/publication/375486065_Gilgamesh_The_Prototypical_Epic_Hero

2

Plato's Tenth Muse: "Now, I Will Sing This Beautifully"

"Some say the Muses are nine: how careless! Look, there's Sappho too, from Lesbos, the tenth!" exclaimed Plato (427–347 BCE) in a much-quoted epigram from the *Anthologia Palatina* (9.506). Well-known in antiquity, Sappho (ca. 570–625 BCE) was lauded as one of the greatest lyric poets, the Poetess incarnate to Homer's Poet. The *Suda*, a Byzantine encyclopedia from the 10th century that included accounts by ancient Greek scholars, attributed nine "books", viz., papyrus scrolls, to Sappho (Rayor and Lardinois 2023). Despite this, most of Sappho's oeuvre has been lost: there are short stanzas here, one or two lines there, and isolated words aplenty. "New" fragments of poetry by Sappho were discovered in 2004 and 2014; others may yet be found. In toto, 650 lines of Sappho have survived but only her *Ode to Aphrodite* is complete; now known as Sappho Fragment 1, it extends over seven four-line stanzas. Understandably, the more complete poems such as Sappho Fragment 16 and Sappho Fragment 31 attract the bulk of scholarly commentary. Not surprisingly, complete works of Sappho showcase more introductions and notes than original text.

Sappho's poems were composed in Aeolic Greek, a pitch-accented dialect from the north-eastern part of Greece encompassing Boeotia, Thessaly, Lesbos, and the Greek colony of Aeolis in modern-day Anatolia. The so-called "Sapphic stanza," a four-line verse form, comprises three metrically identical lines of 11 syllables each, followed by a fourth line of just five syllables (Poets.org, n.d.). The first three lines of the Sapphic stanza are driven by two trochees (a stressed syllable followed by an unstressed one), a dactyl (a stressed syllable followed by two unstressed ones), and then two

© The Author(s), under exclusive license to Springer Nature Singapore Pte Ltd. 2025
O. Serrat, *Myth, Philosophy, and Literature*,
https://doi.org/10.1007/978-981-95-2897-4_2

more trochees; the shorter fourth line is composed of one dactyl followed by a trochee (Poets.org, n.d.). The strict and repetitive meter of the Sapphic stanza, with its starts and stops, builds up an emotion that the language serves to intensify (Poets.org, n.d.).

In addition to introducing the Sapphic stanza, Sappho also innovated poetry through first-person narration, because of which her compositions have been treated as autobiographical (Brooklyn Museum, n.d.). Sappho offered deeply personal and contemporary reflections on *eros* (love), *eris* (strife), yearning, religion, passion, love, loss, lifestyle, family, aging, and the passing of time; she conveyed her feelings with simplicity of thought, clarity and spontaneity of language, sharp and vivid images, intimacy, and endearing honesty. Because she so eloquently championed the innermost self, Sappho is recognized as the first female literary voice in the Western tradition (Greene 1996). Consider Sappho Fragment 42: "Their hearts grew cold/and their wings fell slack" (as translated by Rayor and Lardinois 2023, p. 53); Sappho Fragment 47: "Love shook my senses,/like wind crashing on mountain oaks" (as translated by Rayor and Lardinois 2023, p. 56); Sappho Fragment 52: "I don't expect to touch heaven …" (as translated by Rayor and Lardinois 2023, p. 57); Sappho Fragment 147: "I say someone in another time will remember us" (as translated by Rayor and Lardinois 2023, p. 98); and Sappho Fragment 154: "As the full moon rose,/women stood round the altar" (as translated by Rayor and Lardinois 2023, p. 100). Solon (ca. 630–560 BCE), the statesman who is credited with having laid the foundations of Athenian democracy and a poet himself to boot, was asked why he wanted to be taught a certain poem by Sappho: "Because once I've learned it, I can die," Solon answered (Mendelsohn 2015, para. 1).

Little is known about Sappho's life. Therefore, books and articles about Sapho typically cover similar ground in respect of the 650 lines. What more might one say? Well, Sapho's treasure is hidden in plain sight: the "lyric" in lyric poetry must be taken literally (Mendelsohn 2015, para. 3). Much as the songs of Homer and others, Sappho's poetry was written to be sung and accompanied by the lyre, a stringed instrument like a small harp, as suggested by Sappho Fragment 118: "Come, divine lyre, speak to me/and sing!" (as translated by Rayor and Lardinois 2023, p. 92). Sappho is most closely associated with the barbiton (or barbitos), a lyre-like string instrument that was deep in pitch. One of the earliest surviving images of Sappho, from ca. 470 BCE, on a terracotta kalathos currently held by the State Collections of Antiquities in Munich, Germany, shows her holding a barbiton and plectrum and listening to Alcaeus (ca. 620–580 BCE), another lyric poet from

Lesbos, seemingly preparing to answer his song with hers. Music and poetry are two distinct art forms but connecting them significantly enhances emotional resonance.

Sappho was a singer-songwriter and performed in public much as, say, Bob Dylan, Leonard Cohen, John Lennon, Paul McCartney, Don McLean, and Paul Simon did (Mendelsohn 2015, para. 3). Accepting she may well have improvised melodies, Sappho's music is lost and how she performed, and perhaps also danced, is unknown. Noting that ancient authors loved to recite lines of Sappho's work, Mendelsohn (2015, para. 3) pondered whether they were also hearing certain melodies in their heads. Be that as it may, there is more: D'Angour (2018) explained how, having found fragments of actual melodic notation and reconstructed well-preserved Greek instruments such as the aulos, viz., two double-reed pipes played in pairs by a single performer, scholars have begun to reliably interpret ancient Greek music. D'Angour (2018) underscored that rhythms were central to ancient song and that they can be derived from the meters of the poetry, based strictly on the durations of syllables of words. With Greek instruments, improvised accompaniments to the fragmented remains of Plato's Tenth Muse would justly make music with words in the spirit of Sappho Fragment 160: "Now, I will sing this beautifully/to delight my companions" (as translated by Rayor and Lardinois 2023, p. 101).

References

Brooklynn Museum. (n.d.) Sappho. https://www.brooklynmuseum.org/eascfa/din ner_party/place_settings/sappho

D'Angour A (2018, July 31) Ancient Greek music: Now we finally know what it sounded like. The Conversation. https://theconversation.com/ancient-greek-music-now-we-finally-know-what-it-sounded-like-99895

Greene E (Ed.) (1996) Reading Sappho: contemporary approaches, University of California Press

Mendelsohn D (2015 March 12) Hearing Sappho. The New Yorker. https://www.newyorker.com/books/page-turner/hearing-sappho

Poets.org (n.d.) Sapphic. In: Poets.org. https://poets.org/glossary/sapphic.

Rayor D, Lardinois A (2023) Sappho: a new translation of the complete works. Cambridge University Press

3

Quid Pro Quo with the Gods: Anthropomorphism in Hesiod's *Theogony*

Hesiod's *Theogony*, an epic poem of 1,022 lines composed ca. 730–700 BCE, is the most ambitious rendering of the origin and genealogy of the gods of the Greek pantheon (Pollard and Adkins 2023). The *Theogony* traces the creation and ordering of the universe as generations of gods come into being and culminates with the ascension of Zeus to absolute rule (Kapach 2023). Framed by a fiery cycle of divine births, usurpations, and successions, the *Theogony* is a foundational work of Western literature and religion driven by a universalizing impulse to articulate reality (Kapach 2023). Hesiod meant to awe the reader, better, the listener of early oral transmissions. The subliminal assumption in the *Theogany* was that the listener or reader would connect and, ideally, associate with the travails of gods. Stoddard (2004) demonstrated that Hesiod's claim to profound and miraculous knowledge, well-served by some narrative tricks of the trade (i.e., anachrony, attributive discourse, character text, commentary, embedded focalization), manipulated the audience to believe the revelation in the *Theogony*. At first remove, Stoddard's (2004) explanation was accurate; however, Stoddard (2004) underplayed the role that anthropomorphism played in boosting cognitive and neuropsychological appreciation of the *Theogony* (Zelinová and Škvrnda 2023).

Derived from ancient Greek *ánthrōpos* (ἄνθρωπος, "human") and *morphē* (μορφή, "form, shape"), anthropomorphism connotes with the attribution of human characteristics (e.g., actions, forms, traits) to non-human entities such as animals or deities: put simply, it is the interpretation of events, or things, in terms of human characteristics (Aslan 2017; Guthrie 2023; Psychology Today 2023). The gods of the Greek pantheon were an illustrative case in point: portrayed as

© The Author(s), under exclusive license to Springer Nature Singapore Pte Ltd. 2025
O. Serrat, *Myth, Philosophy, and Literature*,
https://doi.org/10.1007/978-981-95-2897-4_3

men or women, they manifestly shared—even if in extreme forms—commonalities with human beings, viz., positive qualities such as beauty, enhanced intelligence, and power on a good day; earthly vices such as jealousy, lust, and uncontrollable anger on a bad one. True, some so-called minor gods were theriomorphic, from Ancient Greek *thēríon* (θηρίον, "animal") and *morphē* (μορφή, "form, shape"), and had the shapes of beasts (e.g., Achelous, Pan). Irrespective, all the gods had corporeal forms and attendant prototypically human motivations, be they biological, environmental (especially social), or psychological. And so, anthropomorphism would also have the opposing forces of *eros* (the mischievous god of love) and *eris* (the goddess or personified spirit of contention, discord, rivalry, and strife) characterize the affairs of gods.

Psychologists have linked anthropomorphism to humankind's craving for reciprocity: one offers gifts to a god (e.g., prayers, sacrifices) and one expects certain things in return (e.g., successful enterprise) (Airenti 2018; Psychology Today 2023). For instance, the very practical—indeed, almost contractual—Latin expression for the Romans' relationship with the gods was *do ut des* ("I give, so that you may give") (Hellenic Faith 2023). Is this because the ancient Greeks led toilsome lives? Another work of Hesiod, *Works and Days*, also alludes to human suffering. In *Works and Days*, a didactic poem of 828 lines composed ca. 700 BCE, Zeus had warned Prometheus before unleashing Pandora:

> Iapetos' boy, if you're not the smartest of them all!
> I bet you're glad you stole fire and outfoxed me.
> But things will go hard for you and for humans after this.
> I'm going to give them Evil in exchange for fire,
> Their very own Evil to love and embrace. (Trzaskoma et al 2016, p. 163)

In the *Theogony*, the ancient Greeks have no time for abstractions, let alone elemental divinities: they want to act or, at least, interact to satisfy their needs and desires. The *Theogony* is violently human: Cronus castrates Uranus and swallows his own children before being defeated by Zeus. In the *Theogony*, the world is harsh and the gods are predominantly cruel. *The Epic of Gilgamesh* (with first accounts composed as far back as ca. 2100 BCE) and *Genesis* (composed around 1450–1400 BCE) likewise evoke the tenuous nature of the earliest settled societies.

Hypothetically, therefore, the disconsolate anthropomorphism in the *Theogony* can be explained by the circumstances that prevailed at the time of the poem's appearance. Hesiod lived in the early Greek Archaic period of history (ca. 800–480 BCE): there were developments in architecture, arts and crafts (including pottery and sculpture), politics, scientific thinking, storytelling, technology, and writing (with the introduction of the Greek alphabet), presumably stimulated by Mediterranean Sea trade and coinage. Even so, the *Theogony* reflects the Greek Dark Age (ca. 1200–800 BCE) and the decline of Bronze Age civilizations (Mark 2023). All the same, change was afoot: Homer's *Iliad*, another epic poem of 15,693 lines composed ca. 760–710 BCE, was given over to humans. The gods still play important roles in *The Iliad*, and much text continuingly imparts that humankind is born to bear in action and interaction with the gods; but, Homer let its human protagonists stake their place in the world and shape it to their belligerent ends in a subtler quid pro quo with the gods even if *moira* (μοῖρα)—"individual destiny," "the will of the gods," "fate"—has predetermined all. The travails of Achilles, one of the great heroes of Greek mythology and a half-god himself, are existential in the highest. Does *The Iliad* intimate that the inability of humans to accept destiny is, paradoxically, what makes destiny come to pass? Put differently, do we make our miseries transpire by our own deeds? Paradoxical as it may sound in a world governed by *moira* (μοῖρα), the moral responsibility of protagonists is a major theme in *The Iliad* (Janko 1992).

The conception of gods in human terms was ultimately challenged: Xenophanes (ca. 560–478 BCE), the earliest known social critic of anthropomorphism, delivered trenchant attacks on the immorality of the gods in the Greek pantheon (Guthrie 2023). Socrates (ca. 470–399 BCE) particularized his criticism of dissolute exploits: Hesiod, Homer, and other poets were to blame for telling tales in which gods—and so-called heroes—set a bad example (Morales 2007): he was accused of corruptive behavior, put on trial, and executed. Still, Xenophanes, Socrates, and others such as Euripides (ca. 480–406 BCE) helped propagate monotheism (Guthrie 2023). This is not to say anthropomorphism is dead: here and there, people continue to attribute agency to natural events. "Si Dieu nous a faits à son image, nous le lui avons bien rendu," quipped Voltaire (Voltaire 1883, p. 151). ("If God created us in his image, we certainly paid him back.")

References

Airenti G (2018) The development of anthropomorphism in interaction: intersubjectivity, imagination, and theory of mind. Frontiers in Psychology 5(9):1–13

Aslan R (2017) God: a human history. Random House

Guthrie S (2023, August 18) Anthropomorphism. In Encyclopedia Britannica, Retrieved September 20, 2023, from https://www.britannica.com/topic/anthropomorphism

Hellenic Faith (2023). Sacrifice & Do ut des. https://hellenicfaith.com/do-ut-des/

Janko R (1992) The Iliad: a commentary. Cambridge University Press

Kapach A (2023, March 17). Theogony. In Mythopedia. Retrieved September 20, 2023, from https://mythopedia.com/topics/theogony

Mark J (2023, July 27). Greek dark age. In World history encyclopedia. Retrieved September 20, 2023, from https://www.worldhistory.org/Greek_Dark_Age/

Morales H (2007) Classical mythology: a very short introduction. Oxford University Press

Pollard J, Adkins A (2023, April 26). Greek mythology. In Encyclopedia britannica. Retrieved September 20, 2023, from https://www.britannica.com/topic/Greek-mythology

Psychology Today. (2023). Anthropomorphism. https://www.psychologytoday.com/us/basics/anthropomorphism

Stoddard K (2004) The narrative voice in the Theogony of Hesiod. Brill

Trzaskoma S, Smith R, Brunet S, Palaima T (2016) Anthology of classical myth: primary sources in translation, 2nd edn. Hackett Publishing Company

Voltaire (1883) Le sottisier. Garnier

Zelinová Z, Škvrnda F (2023) Anthropomorphic motifs in ancient Greek ideas on the origin of the cosmos. Human Affairs 33(2):172–183. https://doi.org/10.1515/humaff-2022-1003

4

The Three Faces of Thucydides

Thucydides (ca. 460–ca. 395 BCE), a former general who wrote an account of the Peloponnesian War (431–404 BCE) between Athens and Sparta, theorized the writing of history with claims to have applied strict standards of evidence-gathering and impartiality before examining causation (Thucydides 1998). Thucydides left gods and religious explanations out of his writings. While never naming Herodotus (ca. 484–ca. 425 BCE)—his immediate predecessor and so-called "father of history"—and by implication also Homer (ca. 8th century BCE), Thucydides charged earlier historians with fabulation and storytelling. Composed with future ages in mind, not the pleasure of a fleeting moment, Thucydides purported his work to be "a possession for all time" (Thucydides 1998, p. 14).

Thucydides was anointed "father of scientific history" by his contemporaries, Roman historians, and innumerable others including Nietzsche who, thirsting for "reality," accepted his methods, interpretations, and claims (University of Bristol, n.d.). Thucydides' analysis of the internal politics, dynamics, and interrelations of Greek cities revolutionized Western historiography and shaped understandings of politics and international relations across time and space. With the advent of the Cold War, interest in Thucydides surged: in 1947, the American Secretary of State George Marshall compared the struggle between Athens and Sparta to the contest between the United States and the Soviet Union and their respective allies (Kagan 2009a). Might there be a case for also dubbing Thucydides the "father of political history" (Wilson Quarterly 2010)?

"Which Thucydides can you trust?", Beard (2014) asked: "[The *History of the Peloponnesian War*] has regularly been plundered for courses in political

© The Author(s), under exclusive license to Springer Nature Singapore Pte Ltd. 2025
O. Serrat, *Myth, Philosophy, and Literature*,
https://doi.org/10.1007/978-981-95-2897-4_4

theory and international relations, and for the slogans that have supported either a neoconservative or realist, or sometimes even left-wing, political agenda" (Beard 2014, p. 34). There seems to be three faces of Thucydides: the first is his own, stylistic warts and all; the second comes in the form of historiographical critiques of the original; and the third is what neoconservative pundits have latterly affixed on him.

- **The First Face of Thucydides.** Thucydides was at first a general: in 424 BCE, Athens sent him to Thrace to defend the region. However, Thucydides could not prevent Brasidas, a Spartan general, from capturing Amphipolis in the winter of 424–423 BCE. Amphipolis was a colony of considerable importance to Athens: Thucydides was accused of gross negligence and sent into exile for 20 years. To a general, the indictment must have trumped the punishment: could Thucydides have conceived the *History of the Peloponnesian War* to exculpate himself with post-facto demonstration of strategic acumen? Thucydides wrote for 30 years, interviewing participants in the events he recorded and assiduously consulting written documents. Many have read the *History of the Peloponnesian War* as an objective piece of history (Bury and Meiggs 1975); others have seen in Thucydides a skilled artist who selected and arranged his material for symbolic and emotional potential (Connor 1984). But, the scientific rigor of Thucydides returned with a vengeance. Thucydides made extensive use of speeches to elaborate on events he did not attend. In support of what he felt might have been needed on any given occasion, Thucydides probably wrote the speeches in the *History of the Peloponnesian War*, as in the case of the renowned funeral oration of Pericles (Thucydides 1998, pp. 91–97).
- **The Second Face of Thucydides.** Thucydides keeps being dissected. To Greenwood (2005), for example, literary analysis of the speeches suggest Thucydides was exploring how history might be communicated more accurately; and so, the *History of the Peloponnesian War* ought to be considered a work of theory. Quite differently, Kagan (2009b) focused on the quality and reliability of the *History of the Peloponnesian War*. Kagan (2009b) intended to show that Thucydides' take on events was partial in numerous respects, suggesting revisionism. Kagan (2009b) remarked that:

The purpose of Thucydides was to set before us the truth as he saw it, but his truth need not be ours. If we are to use his history with profit, as we can and must, we must distinguish between the evidence he presents and the interpretation he puts on it. (p. 234)

- **The Third Face of Thucydides.** Seventy years later, the Marshall band-wagon plays on. The eponymous Thucydides Trap proposes to explain U.S.–China relations in the twenty-first century with reference to the pattern of structural stress that ensues when an emerging power looks to displace a hegemon (Allison 2017). Manifestly, the Thucydides Trap ignores the sundry biological, psychological, and social reasons why wars occur: it overplays the security dilemma, which posits that an increase in one state's security leads other states to fear for their own, even though states harbor ambitions beyond security (Wolf 2017); and, it focuses on structural determinism and escalation to the detriment of leadership and political agency (Platias and Trigkas 2021). Shelving "event-based" approaches to history, Braudel (1949) argued long ago that demography, geography, and social and economic developments were more telling.

The foregoing is par for the course. *Pace* Thucydides' scientific pretentions, why did anyone ever expect a history book to be free of intent?

> Historians are not just dispassionate chroniclers. By their selection, ordering, highlighting, attribution, and analysis of facts they fashion a particular version of the past. And they also play a part in the disputes of the present, by legitimizing or undermining the rationales, heroes, and myths which influence current debates. Historical figures are forever being conscripted for fresh cultural battles. (The Times, 2002, as cited in Age of the Sage, n.d.)

With hubris, Thucydides wanted his work to be a possession for all time. In the very same contentious world that he wanted to elucidate, it is as if the gods whom Thucydides belittled have had historians and strategists enlist him in the ranks; they now march Thucydides hither and thither to explain everything and nothing.

References

Age of the Sage (n.d.) Quotes about historiography. https://www.age-of-the-sage.org/history/quotations/historiography.html

Allison G (2017) Destined for war: can America and China escape Thucydides' trap?. Houghton Mifflin Harcourt

Beard M (2014) Confronting the classics. Profile Books

Braudel F (1949) La Méditerranée et le monde méditerranéen à l'époque de Philippe II. Armand Colin

Bury J, Meiggs R (1975) A history of Greece to the death of Alexander the Great. Macmillan

Connor W (1984) Thucydides. Princeton University Press

Greenwood E (2005) Thucydides and the shaping of history. Bristol Classical Press

Kagan D (2009a) The student of political behavior. The New Criterion. https://newcriterion.com/issues/2009/9/the-student-of-political-behavior

Kagan D (2009b) Thucydides: the reinvention of history. Penguin Books

Platias A, Trigkas V (2021) Unravelling the Thucydides' Trap: inadvertent escalation or war of choice? Chin J Int Politics 14(2):219–255

Thucydides (1998) The Peloponnesian war. (Trans: Lattimore S). Hackett Publishing Company, Inc

University of Bristol. (n.d.) Thucydides—still relevant today? https://www.bristol.ac.uk/research/impact/thucydides/

Wilson Quarterly (2010) The father of political history. Wilson Quarterly 34(1):74–75. https://www.wilsonquarterly.com/quarterly/_/the-father-of-political-history

Wolf A (2017, July 25). What Thucydides' trap gets wrong about the United States and China. Modern War Institute. https://mwi.westpoint.edu/thucydidess-trap-gets-wrong-united-states-china/

Part II

Epistemologies of Knowledge

5

Bridging Worlds: Comparative Epistemology and the Mind–Body Problem

Ludwig Wittgenstein (1889–1951), an Austrian philosopher, encouraged us to question the assumptions that are embedded in words: "Philosophy is a battle against the bewitchment of our intelligence by means of language," he inferred in appreciation of the nature of language, its relations with the world, and the concepts used to describe and analyze it (Wittgenstein 1953, p. 47). Comparative epistemology is one approach with which to set traditions into dialogue with inclusive vision: by engaging varied cultural, linguistic, and philosophical sources with intellectual humility and respect for particularities, comparative epistemology promotes understanding of differences and similarities to shed light on beliefs, ethics, existence, knowledge, and truth. A case in point is comparative epistemology's treatment of the so-called mind–body problem in the Western philosophy of mind, an enduring debate about the connections between consciousness, physicality, and existence.

5.1 The Mind–Body Problem

Using The Allegory of the Cave, in which men who have been confined by chains all their lives perceive reality through shadows that are cast by objects in front of a fire, Plato (427–347 BCE), a Greek philosopher, contended in *The Republic* (Plato 2003) that humankind is fettered by mental "chains" and limited understanding of the world. Plato (2003) suggested that we should use intellect if we are to better grasp reality and create a better society.

O. Serrat, *Myth, Philosophy, and Literature,*
https://doi.org/10.1007/978-981-95-2897-4_5

According to Plato (2003), there exists a perfect, eternal world of "forms" that transcends the physical world we experience: "forms" are absolute, non-physical, timeless, and unchangeable, and the physical world we inhabit including its objects are mere—but constantly transforming—imitations. Plato (2003) believed that true knowledge is the ability to grasp the "forms" and distinguished such knowledge from mere opinion. *The Republic* (Plato 2003) was about true knowledge, to be acquired by education, as well as its role in society and the just city-state. Plato's dualistic perspective reached full expression in *Phaedo* (Plato 2009), also known to ancient readers as *On the Soul*, in which he likened the body to a prison in which the soul is confined. Plato (2009) argued that the soul is immortal: it enters the body at birth, leaves it at death, and continues to exist in the afterlife; the soul—not the body—is the seat of reason, knowledge, and wisdom.

Continuing in the same vein, René Descartes (1596–1650), a French mathematician, philosopher, and scientist, proposed that perfect knowledge can be derived if one separates the mind from the body. Descartes' (2004, 2008) axiology (or theory of value) was the pursuit of certain knowledge; his ontology (or science of being) centered on the dualism of mind and body, the first being a thinking, non-extended thing and the second being an extended, non-thinking thing; and, his epistemology (or theory of knowledge) held that perfect knowledge can be derived through doubt and reason. Descartes (2004, 2008) admitted mind–body interaction: the mind can cause the body to move and the body's senses carry information about the environment to cause sensations in the mind. Nonetheless, Descartes (2004, 2008) insisted that, despite their unity in forming a human being, mind and body are existentially separable: matter is spatial and characterized by linear dimensions (i.e., depth, height, length, position); mental entities lack such characteristics. Positing that their properties are irreconcilable, Descartes (2004, 2008) explored a perceived gap between the material body and the immaterial mind.

Fueling tension between Christian theology and science, the mind–body problem that Descartes (2004, 2008) framed has remained a central concern of Western philosophy with intricate connections to epistemology. Descartes lived in an intellectually vibrant time: reactions to the mind–body problem gave rise to empiricism, which contrary to Cartesian rationalism asserted that knowledge is born of experience and observation (Locke 1690). Even so, Descartes' method of doubt provided an ultimate epistemic authority with which to buttress scientific inquiry and assess knowledge claims: rationalism—and the breaking down of complex systems into simpler parts that it encouraged—shaped the intellectual landscape of the 17th and the 18th centuries with omnipresent applications to this day (Serrat 2017a, 2017b). In the fullness of time, Gilbert Ryle (1900–1976) a British philosopher who subscribed to Wittgenstein's philosophy of language, contested the affirmation that the mind exists alongside but is separate from the body, sparking in Western philosophy a discussion around "knowing that" (or propositional knowledge) and "knowing how" (or procedural knowledge) (Ryle 1946). One may wonder if Ryle ever perceived a connection between his epistemological categories and the mind–body problem. Then, with implications for agency, the mind–body problem again entered the fray in the 1990s on account of advancements in the physical sciences, especially functional magnetic resonance imaging and positron emission tomography. Agency denotes an individual's ability to act autonomously and make unrestricted decisions: in the context of the mind–body problem, it is tied to the question of mental causation and how mental states can lead to physical action. Relatedly, materialism (or modern physicalism) seeks to solve what Chalmers (1995, 1996), an Australian cognitive scientist and philosopher, termed the "hard problem" of consciousness (e.g., imaginations, memories, perceptions, sensations, thoughts). The "hard problem" is the enigma of how consciousness emerges from neural activity to navigate, at times in ordered sequence and at other times in chaotic fashion, the relationship between mind and body.

To note, even if Descartes' exploration of the realization of the self ("I think, therefore I am") compares with the Buddhist concept of self-awareness or mindfulness, his axiology, ontology, and epistemology contrast with Buddhist and Chinese cultural, linguistic, and philosophical sources such as the *Tao Te Ching* and the *Zhuangzi* (Watson 2013). Generally, the axiology of Buddhist and Chinese traditions prioritizes harmony, balance, and the interconnectedness of things. Generally, also, the ontology of Buddhist and Chinese traditions proposes that reality is interdependent and constantly changing, leading in Daoism to acceptance that the "way" is the natural order of the universe and in Buddhism to the concept of "emptiness", whereby all phenomena are devoid of inherent existence. Furthermore, the epistemology of Buddhist and Chinese traditions values experiential knowledge (i.e., "knowing how"), its skillful application, and intuitive understanding in line with Daoism's emphasis on the "path" and "effortless action" in a world defined by "self-causation". Daoism's epistemology was presumed to conduce ethical action and social harmony. In the absence of theoretical sciences providing explanations of the natural world and the universe, barring astronomy and mathematics in ancient India and astronomy in China, there was little room for Descartes' (2004, 2008) systematic doubt and formal logic: in Buddhist and Chinese traditions, inductive reasoning founded in experience of the world and analogical logic based on given statements and similar consequences from past experiences were preferred. This not to say Eastern traditions are inimical to science. Bertrand Russell (1872–1970), a British logician, mathematician, and philosopher, deemed Buddhism to be a speculative and scientific philosophy that could bridge in Western philosophy the estranged worlds of matter and spirit (Russell 2004). More recently, the 14th Dalai Lama [Tenzin Gyatso] has verbalized that "Buddhism is more than a religion. It is a science of the mind" (2006). Inevitably, therefore, the modern debate in Western philosophy about the mind–body problem has drawn Buddhism into its disputes.

5.2   The Mind–Body Problem in Modern Debate

Neuroscience is the study of the structure and function of the nervous system and brain. Taking advantage of breakthroughs in neuroscience (e.g., mapping brain function, decoding decision-making), materialism contends that conscious experience is nothing more than a brain activity.

5.2.1 The Advent of Materialism

Daniel Dennett (1942–2024), an American cognitive scientist and philosopher, was a self-declared atheist, materialist, and reductionist who, in *Consciousness Explained* (Dennett 1991), asserted that "Somehow the brain must be the mind" (p. 41) and that materialism is "a received opinion approaching unanimity" (p. 106). From autodidactic forays into the fields of artificial intelligence and neuroscience, Dennett (1991) concluded that nothing but information passes into the brain through the senses and the brain's activity is in turn nothing but information processing; and so, as said by Dennett (1991), only by being informed by science could one have a productive philosophical debate about the mind–body problem. In 2009, an exchange between Dennett and Alvin Plantinga, an American Christian philosopher, was published under the grand title of *Science and Religion: Are They Compatible?* (Dennett and Plantinga 2011). Structured as a dialogue, with each protagonist presenting his views and then responding to the other's line of reasoning, Dennett and Plantinga (2011) had Dennett profess from a naturalistic perspective that science offers a complete explanation of our existence without the need for religious belief; from a theistic perspective, Plantinga averred that belief in God is compatible with evolutionary theory and that religion and science are compatible. Dennett and Plantinga (2011) featured caustic rhetoric from Dennett who tasked Plantinga "to show why his theist story deserves any more respect or credence than" "Supermanism" (p. 28), a theme that Dennett revisited throughout the dialogue. The gist of Plantinga's argument was that "contemporary evolutionary theory is compatible with theistic belief" (Dennett and Plantinga 2011, p. 3) because if evolution had been unguided "the chances are we'd get creatures of very different sorts from the ones actually present on earth" (Dennett and Plantinga, p. 5). "Plantinga's story was first assembled in an age of scientific ignorance [. . .]", Dennett retorted (Dennett and Plantinga 2011, p. 47) before asserting that Plantinga's belief depends on miracles happening. Plantinga volunteered that atheism might be less compatible with evolution than Christian theism, admonishing that "[p]erpetuating the myth that there is conflict [. . .] is harmful to religion and to science" (Dennett and Plantinga 2011, p. 70). Replete with "knowing that", Dennett and Plantinga (2011) exemplified the turning of deaf ears.

Starting in the mid-1980s, Paul and Patrica Churchland, two Canadian philosophers, were quick to leverage neuroscience in support of their work on the mind–body problem (MacFarquhar 2007). The Churchlands asserted that the best way to understand the mind was to study the brain. In *Neurophilosophy: Toward a Unified Science of the Mind–Brain* (Churchland 1986), Patricia Churchland rejected the view that consciousness is a mystery that science should not touch and asserted that mental states are brain states, taking arms against Wittgenstein's *bon mot* apropos the role of language. For Patricia Churchland, as noted by Baggini (2019), philosophers cast spells by being so focused on concepts that they neglect to explore the world. "*Consciousness* [emphasis in original], almost certainly, is not a semimagical glow emanating from the soul or permeating spooky stuff. It is, very probably, a coordinated pattern of neuronal activity serving various biological functions. This does not mean that consciousness is not real. Rather, it means that its reality is rooted in its neurobiology," wrote Churchland (2002). This may have prompted Tümkaya's (2021) aside that the Churchlands are non-philosophers working in philosophy departments. More radically still, Paul Churchland argued that mental states and processes are nothing more than states and processes of the brain: this implies that the mental can be reduced to the physical and, consequently, that the mind does not exist at all. Paul Churchland's stance is known as eliminative materialism

(Churchland 1981): it is the provocative idea that most mental states in folk (or commonsense) psychology (e.g., beliefs, desires, fear, hope) are mere propositional attitudes. No matter what, however, the mind–body explanations of the Churchlands suffered from over-reliance on neuroscience, a field that is beyond infancy but not yet mature (and was even less so in the early 1980s). Also, from the perspective of evolutionary history, the Churchlands' assumption that there is no basis for the origin of the non-physical mind is not sufficiently developed to justify a dismissal of the existence of the mind. To wit, materialism faces challenges related to two features of mental states, namely, intentionality and phenomenal consciousness. Mental states represent (or are about) external objects, properties, and circumstances and materialism struggles to fully account for them. In addition, phenomenal consciousness has a subjective "what it's like" aspect and materialism also finds it difficult to account for this experience. In closing, despite Patricia Churchland's comments about Wittgenstein's insight, the Churchlands' joint oeuvre is paradoxically another story meaning to make the language of science theirs with "knowing that" of the "Trust me, I know better than you" variety. Stories help us make sense of the world but the mind–body problem is multifaceted: it has challenged philosophers for centuries. In place of stories, we need framing that enables new explanations.

5.2.2 The Dalai Lama's Rejoinder

For long, the 14th Dalai Lama has maintained that Buddhism, a non-theistic philosophical tradition with perhaps 500 million followers today, shares principles with science including empiricism, reliance on causality, and a suspicion of absolutes (Lama 2005). *The Universe in a Single Atom* (Lama 2005) explored the intersection between religion and science: it recognized their uneasy coexistence but signified they cannot be at cross-purposes since both grapple with the nature of reality. Even-handedly, Lama (2005) gave words of advice to the two communities. Spiritual practitioners can fall into fundamentalism if they do not integrate the study of science into their worldview, Lama (2005) forewarned. That said, "Buddhism accords greatest authority to experience, with reason second and scripture last," Lama (2005, p. 24) avowed, implicitly refuting Descartes' (2004, 2008) argument that reason primes all. Besides, "[both science and Buddhism] share a strong empirical basis: if science shows something to exist or to be non-existent (*which is not the same thing as not finding it*) [emphasis added], then [Buddhism] must accept this as a fact," Lama (2005, p. 24) continued, in what might also be read as a "Physician, heal thyself" (Latin: *Medice, cura te ipsum*) reflection on science's pretensions. Parenthetically also, Lama (2005, p. 24) may be read as writing off Dennett's rationale for deriding Plantinga's theistic story in Dennett and Plantinga (p. 28). Subtly, *The Universe in a Single Atom* (Lama 2005) put forward that "[Science] does not and cannot exhaust all aspects of reality, in particular the nature of human existence" (p. 39): "Reality, including our own existence, is so much more complex than objective scientific materialism allows" (p. 39). Appropriately, given the role of neuroscience and the use that the materialists have made of it, *The Universe in a Single Atom* (Lama 2005) flagged the study of consciousness as an renewed area of investigation. Consciousness is a defining characteristic of sentience, Lama (2005) reminded us: accordingly, it is central to Buddhist thinking because of Buddhism's "primary interest in questions of ethics, spirituality, and overcoming suffering" (p. 121). Lama (2005) acknowledged that neuroscience has made progress in understanding the workings of the brain and the mechanisms that underly consciousness. Nevertheless, Lama (2005) underscored the importance of subjective experiences and the need to incorporate them into scientific discourse, "[else] we risk objectifying what is essentially an internal set of experiences and excluding the necessary presence of the experiencer. We cannot remove ourselves from the equation" (p. 122). The point of Lama (Lama 2005) was that the mind is best studied by a mix of first- and third-person methods. By integrating ethics, responsibility, and commonsense as it did, Lama's (2005) position could not be further away from that of the materialists. Fructifying Buddhist and Daoist epistemology, notably "knowing how", Lama (2005) concluded that by combining scientific findings with introspective practices derived from spiritual traditions, such as the practice of mindfulness, we can gain a more comprehensive understanding of the mind. "I believe that it is possible for Buddhism and modern science to engage in collaborative research in the understanding of consciousness while leaving aside the philosophical question of whether consciousness is ultimately physical" (Lama 2005, p. 137).

5.2.3 Misappropriated: Buddhism and Science

Owen Flanagan, an American professor of neurobiology and philosophy, has worked at the intersection of moral philosophy, neuroscience, and religion in a relatively new philosophical niche: naturalized ethics. In philosophy, naturalism is the belief that everything arises from natural causes and spiritual and supernatural explanations are discounted or excluded. From that perspective,

Flanagan (2011) aimed to examine the possibility of a "naturalized" Buddhism, a "*tame* kind of Buddhism" [emphasis added] (p. 59) that—per Flanagan (2011)—would align with empirical evidence and scientific knowledge. It is not easy to reconcile with religious beliefs a worldview that seeks to rationalize everything through natural processes. Perchance, a naturalist and a theist might deliberate the validity of religious experiences, the basis of moral values, and the nature of reality; that would be par for the course. However, Flanagan (2011) read as if it were a philosophical manifesto on "knowing that", peppered with such terms as "superstitious nonsense" (p. 59) and "hocus pocus" (p. 64), intent on arriving at the possibly foregone conclusion that:

> There is no longer any need for bewilderment, befuddlement, or mysterianism from Buddhism or any other great spiritual tradition in the face of the overwhelming evidence that all experience takes place in our embodied nervous systems in the world, the natural world, the only world there is. (Flanagan 2011, p. 90).

From the outset, Flanagan (2011) held forth in the name of science based on "evidence" (p. 65, 79, 86, 87, 90) from the developing field of neuroscience: "The scientific method has shown, and keeps showing, its mettle when it comes to revealing the truth in a way no other method matches" (p. 59). A stratagem in Flanagan's (2011) refutation of Buddhism's proclaimed affinity for science (e.g., empiricism, reliance on causality, suspicion of absolutes) related to Lama's (2015) advice not to conflate the two processes of not finding something and finding its nonexistence. On that subject, Lama (2005) shared a nuanced understanding of perception and reality, suggesting also that our methods of searching or our understanding might be limited, hence the need to keep an open mind. To Flanagan (2011), however, Lama's (2005) advice was a challenge to Flanagan's (2011) particularized application of the scientific method to Buddhism, even though Lama (2005) agreed with falsifiability, viz., the capacity for some hypothesis, proposition, statement, or theory to be proven wrong. Flanagan's objection to Lama's (2005) use of the falsifiability was deliberate but one point of (likely exaggerated) misinterpretation pertained to the concept of a nonphysical "pure luminous consciousness" (pp. 86–88). Flanagan (2011) dismissed Lama's (2005) claim to states of "pure luminous consciousness" to align with material conceptions of the mind by means of neuroscience. Another stratagem in Flanagan's (2011) rejection of Buddhism's proclaimed affinity for science was the dismissal of "pure luminous consciousness". However, in Buddhist philosophy, a "pure luminous consciousness" refers to a subtle, profound state of mind, potentially attainable by all human beings seeking enlightenment, such as may be achieved through meditation to remove the "Three Poisons" (i.e., delusion, greed, hatred) and change one's disposition. "Pure luminous consciousness" is a central concept in Buddhist thought and practice: it proposes that delusion, greed, hatred are not the lot of humanity and that self-transformation is possible. Because consciousness might be inherently self-revealing, giving notice to "pure luminous consciousness" helped Flanagan (2011) to indirectly strike at phenomenology, which detracts from Flanagan's (2011) truth but might find a convergence of interests with neuroscience in the field of neurophenomenology.

5.3   Bridging Worlds: Reconciling Epistemologies

Geoffrey Lloyd, a British historian of ancient science and medicine, revealed that sophisticated studies of the external world were conducted in Mesopotamia, Greece, India, and China long before science as we know it existed (Lloyd 2014). *The Ideals of Inquiry: An Ancient History* (Lloyd 2014) showed that early studies of the external world delved on methods, viz., how should explorations be pursued; subject matter, viz., what assumptions were to be made about the phenomena to be explored; and aims and value, viz., what purposes explorations should serve. Transparency and accountability were two ideals of early inquiry (Lloyd 2014). Lloyd (2014) referenced such scientific concepts as axioms, common opinions, demonstration, incontrovertibility, postulates, and persuasion in ancient texts and castigated sixteenth-century Jesuits for not seeing that the process-based five-element theory of the Chinese was superior to their substance-based four-element theory. Contemplating the achievements of the past, Lloyd (2014) queried whether "human reasoning, the faculty, exhibits certain stable and recurrent characteristics across all human populations across time and space, despite the apparent differences in how that reasoning manifests itself" and answered in the affirmative (p. 116). Contrasting uneven scientific progress in ancient traditions, however, Lloyd (2014) showcased "the importance of political ideology, of the existence of institutions supporting learning and research, of the values of the group or the society in question" (p. 131). Lloyd's (2014) central contention, that this précis endorses, was that comparative epistemology helps overcome intellectual blind spots. Just as "knowing that" and "knowing how" need not be a case of either/or, the mind–body problem is important enough to warrant both/and approaches for the benefit of researchers and thence for that of humanity (Serrat 2024).

References

Baggini J (2019, Oct 8) Out of mind: philosopher Patricia Churchland's radical approach to the study of human consciousness. Prospect. https://www.prospectmagazine.co.uk/essays/39305/out-of-mind-philosopher-patricia-churchlands-radical-approach-to-the-study-of-human-consciousness

Chalmers D (1995) Facing up to the problem of consciousness. J Conscious Stud 2:200–219

Chalmers D (1996) The conscious mind: in search of a fundamental theory. Oxford University Press

Churchland P (1981) Eliminative materialism and the propositional attitudes. J Philos 78:67–90

Churchland P (1986) Neurophilosophy: toward a unified science of the mind–brain. MIT Press

Churchland P (2002) Brain-wise: studies in neurophilosophy. MIT Press

Dennett D (1991) Consciousness explained. Little, Brown and Co

Dennett D, Plantinga A (2011) Science and religion: are they compatible? Oxford University Press

Descartes R (2004) A discourse on method: meditations and principles (trans: Veitch J). Orion Publishing Group, (Original work published 1637)

Descartes R (2008) Meditations on first philosophy with selections from the objections and replies (trans: Moriarty M). Oxford University Press, (Original work published 1641)

Flanagan O (2011) The Bodhisattva's brain: buddhism naturalized. MIT Press

Lama D (2005) The universe in a single atom: the convergence of science and spirituality. Harmony

Lama D (2006, Nov 6) Buddhism is a science of the mind: Dalai Lama. His Holiness the 14th Dalai Lama of Tibet. https://www.dalailama.com/news/2006/buddhism-is-a-science-of-the-mind-dalai-lama

Lloyd G (2014) The ideals of inquiry: an ancient history. Oxford University Press

Locke J (1690) An essay concerning human understanding. Thomas Basset

MacFarquhar L (2007, Feb 12). Two heads: a marriage devoted to the mind–body problem. The New Yorker

Plato (2003) The republic (trans: Lee D). Penguin, (Original work written ca. 380 BCE)

Plato (2009) Phaedo. (trans: Gallop D). Oxford University Press. (Original work written ca. 360 BCE

Russell B (2004) Mysticism and logic. Dover Publications, Inc. (Original work published 1917)

Ryle G (1946) Knowing how and knowing that: the presidential address. Proc Aristot Soc 46(1):1–16

Serrat O (2017a) Asking effective questions. In: Knowledge solutions: tools, methods, and approaches to drive organizational performance, Springer, pp 889–895

Serrat O (2017b) Critical thinking. In: Knowledge solutions: tools, methods, and approaches to drive organizational performance, Springer, pp 1095–1100

Serrat O (2024) Knowing that and knowing how: Must it be either/or? Unpublished manuscript, Georgetown University. https://www.researchgate.net/publication/379514661_Knowing_That_and_Knowing_How_Must_It_Be_EitherOr

Tümkaya S (2021) On the proper treatment of the Churchlands. Erkenntnis 86(4):905–918

Watson B (2013) The complete works of Zhuangzi. (trans: Watson B) Columbia University Press, (Original work written ca. 476–221 BCE)

Wittgenstein L (1953) Philosophical investigations (trans: Anscombe G). Blackwell, (Original work published 1953)

6

Knowing That and Knowing How: Must It Be Either/Or?

In 1946, Gilbert Ryle (1900–1976), a British philosopher, delivered a 16-page-long address titled *Knowing How and Knowing That* at a meeting of the Aristotelian Society in London, England. Without explicitly addressing Cartesian thought in his address, Ryle (1946) implicitly challenged the proposition of French philosopher and mathematician René Descartes, first published in 1641, that the concept of the mind exists alongside but separate from the body (Descartes 2008). Ryle's (1946) address was quickly followed by *The Concept of Mind* (Ryle 1949).

Descartes (1596–1650) was a supreme dualist in the vein of Socrates (ca. 470–399 BCE) and Plato (427–347 BCE), whom with Aristotle (384–322 BCE) many consider the fathers of philosophy (Serrat 2017a, 2017b). At the peak of Greece's Classical period (viz., the 5th and 4th centuries BCE), Plato had asserted in *The Republic* (Plato 2003), originally written ca. 380 BCE, that the physical world we know is but a shadow of the real one. Plato had posited two levels of reality: the intelligible world of non-physical, timeless, absolute, and unchangeable essences that Plato termed "forms"; and, the world we inhabit but which only imitates the forms (Plato 2003). Plato (2003) used the allegory of a cave to demonstrate that people are ignorant of the forms and only see shadows, while only a person with wisdom (ideally, a "philosopher-king") can discern the true nature of things. Plato and before him Socrates were suspicious of democracy: they apprehended that, instead of addressing issues rationally, uneducated citizens might be fooled by easy answers.

© The Author(s), under exclusive license to Springer Nature Singapore Pte Ltd. 2025
O. Serrat, *Myth, Philosophy, and Literature*,
https://doi.org/10.1007/978-981-95-2897-4_6

Plato (2003) even castigated artists and poets such as Homer (born ca. 8th century BCE) for being imitators whose creations were far from the truth.

The axiology (or theory of value) of Descartes (2004, 2008) lies in the pursuit of perfect knowledge; in line with that, his ontology (or science of being) focuses on the dualism of mind (viz., spirit or soul) and body while his epistemology (or theory of knowledge) holds that certain knowledge can—from innate ideas—be derived without the aid of the five sensory organs. Along with Descartes (2004, 2008), therefore, we should initially doubt everything to determine whether there is anything we can know with certainty. Illustrating, Descartes (2004, 2008) contended that one has certain knowledge of one's own existence because the very act of thinking proves that one exists. In contrast, John Locke (1632–1704), a British philosopher and physician, was soon after the death of Descartes to publish *An Essay Concerning Human Understanding*, which set the foundations of empiricism (Locke 1690). Refuting the concept of innate ideas, Locke (1690) described the mind at birth as a "blank slate".

Relatedly, Ryle's (1946, 1949) attack on intellectualism differentiated two types of knowledge, viz., "knowing that" (or propositional knowledge) and "knowing how" (or procedural knowledge), before contesting that intelligence—the ability to learn or understand or to deal with new or trying circumstances—finds expression in cognition or intellectual understanding. On the word of Ryle (1946, 1949), "knowing how" connotes skills or operations; in other words, it is the practical knowledge with which to perform actions. To Ryle (1946, 1949), on the other hand, "knowing that" stands for an individual's cognitive repertoire (or factual knowledge), such as knowing that Sussex is a county in England; and so, "knowing that" is the propositional knowledge or understanding that something is the case. Crucially, according to Ryle (1946, 1949), "knowing how" is principally characterized by responsiveness to changes in the conditions under which intelligent behavior takes place; consequently, it is quite different from what Descartes (2004, 2008) had deduced. Summing up, Ryle (1946, 1949) believed that what guides us in action ("knowing how") is a distinct performative capacity from what guides us in reflection ("knowing that"): he argued that the two types of knowledge are naturally completely distinct, suggesting also that the notion about "knowing how" being dependent on "knowing that" leads to an infinite regress, that is, a sequence of reasoning or justification that can never come to an end.

Cartesian thinkers are wont to transcend reality courtesy of supposedly new ways of "knowing that". Rawls (1921–2002), an American philosopher, is a recent case in point. With *The Theory of Justice*, Rawls (1971) aspired to address the problem of distributive justice by way of an alternative to utilitarianism. Rawls (1971) suggested that we should imagine we sit behind a "veil of ignorance" that prevents us from knowing who we are and identifying with our personal circumstances. By being ignorant of our circumstances, Rawls (1971) argued that we can more objectively consider how societies could allow reason to operate maximally; this entails the notion that freeing the mind from the body and material circumstances allows propositional knowledge to emerge. By virtue of such "knowing that", Rawls (1971) argued that society could then be structured so that the greatest possible amount of liberty is given to its members, limited only by the requirement that the liberty of any one member should not infringe upon that of anyone else. Inequalities would only to be allowed if the worst off were better off than they might be under equal distribution; and, if there were beneficial inequality, this inequality should not per Rawls (1971) make it harder for those without resources to occupy positions of power. An aside is warranted given the ambitious compass of Rawls's "knowing that" (Rawls 1971): criticisms of Rawls (1971) have centered on the unacceptability of inequalities, which even if they were to benefit the least advantaged do not maximize utility. Contrarily, libertarians have rationalized that some people deserve certain economic benefits on account of their actions. Rawls (1971) has also been criticized for not being dynamic or evolutionary, not considering uncertainty or the role of chance, and for romanticizing society to the detriment of research into how justice might—to begin—be restored in an unjust society.

Different cultures have approached the nature of knowledge differently and it is of interest to counterpoise "knowing that" and "knowing how" by engaging in comparative (or cultural) philosophy. Buddhist and Chinese sources, for instance, favor the axiology, ontology, and epistemology of "knowing how"; they also surface the tension within the Western tradition of "knowing that", to which philosophers such as Locke (1690) and Ryle (1946, 1949) drew attention. Connected to the (possibly mythical) Chinese philosopher Laozi (born ca. 6th century BCE), also romanized as Lao Tzu, Daoism (Chinese: 道教) is a non-theistic philosophical tradition that has shaped Chinese life for over 2000 years. *Dao* (Chinese: 道) is usually translated as "path" or "way", sometimes as "doctrine" or "technique", but most profoundly as the Cosmic Way (Britanica 2024). Daoism finds expression in *de* (Chinese: 德), which means "excellence", "integrity", or "virtue", especially through *ziran* (Chinese: 自然) and *wuwei* (Traditional Chinese: 無為), that last practice translated as "non-doing" in the sense of "effortless action". *Ziran* is the philosophy of spontaneous self-causation: the term literally means "self-soing" or "so of itself", hence "freely", "naturally", or "spontaneously" (Britanica 2024). *Ziran* is the natural state of the constantly unfolding universe and of all things within it (i.e., animals, humans) when they are allowed to develop in accord with the Cosmic Way (Bruya 2022).

The *Zhuangzi*, the eponymous book of Chinese philosopher Zhuangzi (369–298 BCE), also romanized as Chuang Tzu, is alongside the *Dao De Jing*—the title is more commonly rendered as *Tao Te Ching*—one of the two foundational texts of Daoism (Watson 2013). But, whereas the *Tao Te Ching*—which is usually ascribed to Laozi—can be described as mystical and poetic, the *Zhuangzi* concentrates on universal teachings with often humorous allegories, anecdotes, fables, and parables (Watson 2013). Pointedly, the *Tao Te Ching* advances that ultimate reality cannot be characterized with dichotomous concepts: to understand non-duality, one should embrace apparent contradictions (Deguchi et al. 2021). In like spirit, the axiology, ontology, and epistemology of the *Zhuangzi* could not be more different from those of Descartes (2004, 2008) and other "knowing that" dualists. For sure, the axiology of the *Zhuangzi* is enshrined in its advocacy of a natural and spontaneous way of living: explicitly, the *Zhuangzi* values the harmony and diversity of all things, rebuffs hierarchical distinctions and rigid moral judgments, and points up the joy and freedom of wandering and experiencing the world without fixating on goals (Watson 2013). Unlike that of Descartes (2004, 2008), the ontology of the *Zhuangzi* presents a dynamic and fluid view of reality that transcends understanding because everything undergoes constant change and transformation: hence, abreact propositions cannot capture the fluidity of the world (Watson 2013). Equally antithetical to that of Descartes (2004, 2008), the epistemology of the *Zhuangzi* exposes the biases and limitations of our cognitive faculties and questions the utility of reason and language; more satisfactorily, as said by the *Zhuangzi*, understanding advances from analogy, experience, and intuition, which implies adaptability, flexibility, and provisionality (Watson 2013).

Buddhism, a non-theistic philosophical tradition, was founded by Siddhartha Gautama (ca. 563–483 BCE), a wandering ascetic better known as the Buddha ("the Awakened One") who taught in what is now Nepal. Eschewing esotericism, the Buddha focused pragmatically on suffering (Sanskrit: *duḥkha*) as a fundamental problem of life (Gethin 1998). Precisely, on the way to "knowing how" rather than "knowing that", Buddhism investigated Four Noble Truths: the nature of suffering (Sanskrit: *duḥkha*); the nature of its cause (Sanskrit: *samudaya*); the nature of its cessation (Sanskrit: *nirodha*); and the nature of the path leading to its cessation (Sanskrit: *marga*) (Keown 2013). Despite its single-minded preoccupation with suffering, Buddhism is not a world-denying philosophy: it is a realistic approach to life and how one might live it better. Toward "knowing how", Buddhism offers a middle way for humankind to steer clear of the extremes of annihilationism (belief in eternal torment) and universalism (the belief that everyone will be saved). The Eightfold Path to enlightenment by way of which we are to overcome the three principal defilements (Sanskrit: *kleśa*) of the mind (i.e., delusion, greed, hatred) and reach the cessation of suffering (Sanskrit: *nirvāṇa*) summons us to practice wisdom (Sanskrit: *prajñā*), through right understanding and right resolve; morality (Sanskrit: *śīla*), through right speech, right action, and right livelihood; and meditation (Sanskrit: *samādhi*), through right effort, right mindfulness, and right concentration (Armstrong 2004). With radical metaphysics, Buddhism rejected the prevailing Upanisadic equation of *ātman* (Sanskrit: "breath", "essence, or "soul") with *brahman* (Sanskrit: "ultimate reality"), whereby a constant and unchanging "self" beyond suffering somehow underlay and was the basis for changing experiences; conversely, Buddhism contended that the "self" can be analyzed by way of the five aggregates (Sanskrit: *skandhas*)—or psycho-physical components of beings—that condition an individual's ever-changing existence: the physical body (Sanskrit: *rūpa*); sensations and feelings (Sanskrit: *vedanā*); cognitions (Sanskrit: *saṃjñā*); traits and dispositions (Sanskrit: *saṃskāra*); and consciousness or sentiency (Sanskrit: *vijñāna*) (Keown 2013). Different Buddhist schools of thought, each claiming to represent the Buddha's vision, developed after his death. Mahāyāna (lit. "Great Vehicle") Buddhism, for example, holds that all human beings possess a Buddha-like nature: having attained transcendent awareness, a *bodhisattva* ("essence of enlightenment") can then guide others on the same path for more widespread application of Buddhist "knowing how".

In the 1st century CE, missionaries travelling along trade routes brought Buddhism into China; what resulted is an absorbing example of how belief systems can interact on the subject of "knowing how". The *Zhuangzi* provided terminology for expressing Buddhist ideas in Chinese (Watson 2013). Translations rendered Buddhist concepts (e.g., "emptiness", "mind") into language that paralleled the *Zhuangzi*'s (Watson 2013). It so happened that Buddhism and the *Zhuangzi* already shared practices, such as meditation and the use of negation in cognitive reasoning. Eventually, the "knowing how" of the *Zhuangzi* also helped shape Chan Buddhism, a Chinese blend of Buddhism and Daoism emphasizing focused engagement (or "knowing how") in everyday life that from the 6th century CE spread to neighboring Vietnam and Korea and then Japan (Watson 2013).

Referencing and counterpoising Buddhist, Chinese, and Western sources, this précis articulated an understanding of Ryle's (1946, 1949) distinction between the axiology, ontology, and epistemology of "knowing that" and "knowing how". The first of the modern rationalists, Descartes believed that truth could be discovered by the application of human reason: he laid the groundwork for the debates that fueled the Age of Enlightenment in the 17th and 18th centuries CE. Undeniably, "knowing that" has valuable applications, especially in science. And yet, as Buddhist and Chinese sages appreciated, the world is replete with inconsistency and not all problems can be resolved: to understand reality, one must perforce embrace contradictions by also "knowing how". That is why paraconsistent logic would have us recognize the complementary and synergistic relationship between the two truths of "knowing that" and "knowing how". "It doesn't matter if a cat is black or white, as long as it catches mice," Chinese Communist Party chairman Deng Xiaoping (1904–1997) is alleged to have said. Compatibly with Buddhism and Daoism, Chan Buddhism acknowledged the interdependence and impermanence of phenomenal reality but advocated sustained practical commitment so one might manage that. Matter-of-factly, Deng Xiaoping's apothegm reconciles Ryle's distinction between "knowing that" and "knowing how".

References

Armstrong K (2004) Buddha. Penguin Books

Britanica (2024) Ziran. https://www.britannica.com/topic/ziran

Bruya B (2022) Ziran: the philosophy of spontaneous self-causation. State University of New York Press

Deguchi Y, Garfield J, Priest G, Sharf R (2021) What can't be said: paradox and contradiction in East Asian thought. Oxford University Press

Descartes R (2004) A discourse on method: meditations and principles (trans: Veitch J). Orion Publishing Group, (Original work published 1637)

Descartes R (2008) Meditations on first philosophy with selections from the objections and replies (trans: Moriarty M). Oxford University Press, (Original work published 1641)

Gethin R (1998) The foundations of Buddhism. Oxford University Press

Keown D (2013) A very short introduction to Buddhism. 2nd edn. Oxford University Press

Locke J (1690) An essay concerning human understanding. Thomas Basset

Plato (2003) The republic (trans: Lee D). Penguin, (Original work written ca. 380 BCE)

Rawls J (1971) A theory of justice. Belknap Press

Ryle G (1946) Knowing how and knowing that: the presidential address. Proc Aristot Soc, *46*(1):1–16

Ryle G (1949) The concept of mind. Barnes & Noble

Serrat O (2017a) Asking effective questions. In: Knowledge solutions: tools, methods, and approaches to drive organizational performance, Springer, pp 889–895

Serrat O (2017b) Critical thinking. In: Knowledge solutions: tools, methods, and approaches to drive organizational performance, Springer, pp 1095–1100

Watson B (2013) The complete works of Zhuangzi (trans: Watson B). Columbia University Press, (Original work written ca. 476–221 BCE)

7

Reimagining Knowledge: From Dualism to Pluralistic Epistemologies

7.1 Global Epistemologies Beyond Binaries

In conversations interrogating knowledge, discourse frequently organizes itself into a twofold narrative (Serrat 2024a). On one side, Western philosophy is often lauded for its rigorous commitment to logic, empiricism, and detached rational inquiry—an approach that has long shaped academic discourse and provided a foundational framework for scientific advancement (Russell 1945; Serrat 2017a). In contrast, Buddhist philosophy cultivates a tranquil, reflective approach to existence, encouraging mindfulness, deep contemplation of daily life, and recognition of life's inherent interconnectedness (Hanh 1975). While these dominant paradigms have undeniably galvanized debate, offering a convenient shorthand for engaging with ways of knowing, they only begin to map the vast expanse of humanity's epistemological terrain. Leaning excessively on either the analytical rigor of Western philosophy or the contemplative depth of Buddhist mindfulness not only narrows our view of these traditions' unique contributions but also obscures the spectrum of dynamic epistemologies that can broaden our understanding of knowledge (Serrat 2024b).

Across the world, other traditions offer captivating alternatives that transcend the conventional Western paradigm of rational inquiry and the venerable practices of Buddhist experiential reflection. In doing so, they not only enrich these established frameworks but also expand our epistemological boundaries. *Ubuntu*, a Southern African philosophy, views knowledge as a communal resource—interweaving individual insights into a shared tapestry

O. Serrat, *Myth, Philosophy, and Literature*,
https://doi.org/10.1007/978-981-95-2897-4_7

of understanding (Tutu 1999). Originating among the Akan people of Ghana, *sankofa* underscores the value of reclaiming knowledge from the past to guide present and future action. In Yoruba tradition, mythology, spirituality, and ethics converge through the *ifá* divination system, providing a paradigm for understanding existence, destiny, and moral order. In a similar vein, Indigenous epistemologies throughout the Americas, Australia, and Oceania advance a holistic, embodied engagement with the surrounding world, inviting us to experience reality in its most complete form (Cajete 2000). Concurrently, Islamic thought emphasizes the integration of empirical observation, rooted in direct experience, with profound spiritual insight (Nasr 1964). Furthermore, traditional Indian philosophies—such as Advaita Vedānta—ponder the intricate relationship between perception, consciousness, and existence, challenging us to reconsider the very foundations of knowledge and being (Deutsch 1969).

Together, these multiple approaches beckon us to move beyond restrictive binaries and embrace epistemological inclusivity. Broadening our perspective is not merely an academic exercise; it holds tangible benefits by promising fresh insights for education, cultural practices, and public policy. By threading together these varied strands of thought, we open the door to a deeper, more engaging dialogue about how we understand our world—and how we might better shape it for the future.

7.2 Exploring Alternative Epistemologies

7.2.1 Ubuntu: Knowledge Through Community

African epistemologies summon us to reframe knowledge as a woven tapestry of social interrelations, rather than as a solitary, individual pursuit. Consider the philosophy of *ubuntu*, a cornerstone of many African traditions—especially in Southern Africa, where it is encapsulated in the Nguni adage "I am because we are" (Mbiti 1969, p. 106)—which emphasizes that our identities and wisdom are intrinsically linked to the collective experiences of our communities.

In this view, knowledge is not something an individual gathers in isolation; it is nurtured, shared, and continuously refined within a web of relationships. In many African communities, the gathering of elders under a common tree is more than a tradition—it is a forum where tales of ancestral wisdom and practical know-how—from agricultural practices and ethical conduct to conflict resolution—are passed down through generations (Gyekye 1997). Such exchanges rely not only on shared cultural values but also on the high emotional intelligence of community members, which enables them to interpret and respond to the emotional nuances embedded in these narratives (Serrat 2017b). Similarly, communal storytelling sessions during local festivals allow both young and old to contribute to and absorb a shared narrative that reinforces community values and historical memory (Serrat 2017c).

This collective mode of knowing enables communities to preserve historical memory, adapt cultural practices, and engage in cooperative problem-solving in ways that rigid individualism might overlook. Ramose (1999) expands on this by emphasizing that *ubuntu* is more than a cultural ethos—it also serves as a philosophical foundation that challenges individualistic notions of knowledge. He argues that epistemology in a *ubuntu* framework is intrinsically relational, requiring collective participation in meaning-making. This perspective reframes knowledge as a dynamic, communal experience that fosters interconnectedness and shared responsibility. African epistemologies transcend Western models of objectivity and detached analysis, asserting that learning is an embodied experience interwoven with social rituals, artistic expression, music, and communal celebrations. Such practices underscore the idea that knowledge can only truly flourish when it is shared—a dynamic process that benefits not just the individual but the whole community. Embracing this alternative view not only expands our horizons but also lays the groundwork for educational and policy innovations that honor interconnectedness over isolated achievement. This approach compels us to rethink how we define and value knowledge in our increasingly complex and interwoven global society.

7.2.2 Living Earth: Indigenous Epistemologies of Land, Spirit, and Narrative

Indigenous epistemologies offer a vision of knowing that is inseparable from the land, rooted in ritual, and woven from narratives passed through generations. In these traditions, knowledge emerges from lived experience, not from abstract thought confined to the boundaries of the individual mind. It arises from a living, breathing landscape where every hill, river, and rock carries resonance. Indigenous approaches perceive nature as an active, living presence—imbued with spirit and agency—offering an evocative alternative to views that reduce it to a passive object for observation or exploitation. Cajete (1994) eloquently argues that Indigenous epistemologies demand an education that is inseparable from the natural world, where knowledge is not merely transmitted but is lived, experienced, and—above all—firmly rooted.

Across the Americas, Australia, and beyond, storytelling and ritual form the core of a deeply integrated system of understanding. For instance, Native American oral traditions do more than recount history; they animate the land itself, transforming vast landscapes into dynamic arenas of collective memory and sacred practice (Deloria 1999). The Indigenous concept of *sumak kawsay*—a notion developed among the Quechua communities of Bolivia, Ecuador, and Peru—offers a comprehensive framework where ecological integrity, communal well-being, and spiritual fulfillment are seen as intertwined aspects of life (Gudynas 2011). This idea of "good living" subverts Western metrics of progress and individualism by emphasizing a sustainable, balanced way of coexisting with nature. The cosmologies of the Maya in Central America, which still hold currency in regions such as Belize, Guatemala, and Mexico, articulate nature as a living, revered force—where every forest, mountain, and river is understood to be imbued with sacred vitality, reinforcing a reciprocal relationship between people and their environment. In Australia, Aboriginal Dreamtime narratives encapsulate the origins of the world, offering both spiritual guidance and practical lessons about coexistence with nature (Stanner 1979). In Polynesia—the heart of Oceania—practices such as the Samoan tradition of *fa'a Samoa* highlight communal storytelling sessions where ancestral legends are invoked during gatherings, reinforcing community values and connecting contemporary life with a storied past (Shore 1982). Māori epistemologies in Aotearoa New Zealand, particularly through the principles of *whakapapa* (genealogical ties) and *kaitiakitanga* (environmental guardianship), emphasize a profound relational understanding of nature. The natural world is regarded as an integral part of ancestral lineage—a living relative that warrants both reverence and sustainable stewardship.

These practices upend the familiar Western dichotomy that separates the observer from the observed—unveiling instead a realm where human identity is intricately woven into the cycles of nature and the cosmos. While Buddhism indeed cherishes mindfulness, introspection, and the interdependence of all phenomena—with a primary focus on cultivating individual meditative insight and internal transformation—Indigenous epistemologies steer us toward a broader, more embodied understanding. By centering the sensory experience of place and the sacred rhythms of ritual, Indigenous epistemologies reveal that knowledge is forged not solely through abstract analytical reasoning, but also through intimate, lived connections with our environment and community.

In the Indigenous worldview, every ritual, every narrative, and every reverent interaction with the land serves as a conduit for learning, forging a deeper connection between humanity and nature. This approach not only enhances our global understanding of knowledge but also offers practical insights for rethinking environmental stewardship, cultural continuity, and the ways we educate future generations.

7.2.3 Connecting the Empirical and the Spiritual: Islamic Intellectual Traditions

Islamic thought offers a striking testament to balance—a tradition in which reason and revelation are not opposing forces but interlocking facets of a comprehensive epistemology. In this tradition, empirical inquiry is enriched by spiritual insight, with both elements complementing rather than opposing each other.

Islamic scholars have long championed an approach that privileges both rational analysis and divine guidance (Hoover 2007). Their work reveals that truth is not fragmented into isolated domains; rather, it thrives at the intersections of evidence and inspiration. Among the earliest thinkers, Al-Farabi (approximately 870–950) pioneered the synthesis of rational inquiry with prophetic insight, thereby establishing a unified approach to knowledge that profoundly influenced subsequent Islamic intellectual traditions. Ibn Sina (Avicenna, ca. 980–1037) synthesized Aristotelian logic with metaphysical inquiry, proposing a vision of knowledge that incorporates both empirical observation and transcendent wisdom. Al-Ghazali (1058–1111) emphasized that human reason, while indispensable, reaches its fullest potential when complemented by mystical insight—highlighting the importance of harmonizing logical rigor with spiritual understanding. Ibn Rushd (Averroes, 1126–1198) defended the view that rational inquiry and theological reflection are not mutually exclusive; instead, they mutually reinforce each other, laying the groundwork for a comprehensive method of understanding reality. Ibn Taymiyya (1263–1328) exemplified this enduring approach by merging analytical precision with divine inspiration.

This integrated perspective provides a stimulating counterpoint to more fragmented models of knowledge. While some systems draw a strict boundary between observation and mysticism, the Islamic approach welcomes both. Islamic scholarship offers a wealth of insight into how rational inquiry into the natural world can not only coexist with but also reinforce moral and spiritual commitments (Nasr 1975).

In this view, the discipline of reason serves as a tool for understanding the world, while revelation supplies the ethical compass that guides that understanding toward deeper meaning. By bridging the boundaries between analytical rigor and spiritual wisdom, Islamic intellectual traditions invite us to reimagine knowledge as a holistic process. This balance not only affirms the complementary nature of seemingly opposed methods but also inspires practical reflections on how we structure educational systems, facilitate dialogue, and shape public policy in our interconnected world.

7.2.4 Unity in Plurality: Indian Philosophical Traditions Beyond Buddhism

Indian thought is multifaceted: it is not a monolithic doctrine. While Buddhism significantly informs our understanding of Indian epistemology, traditions like Advaita Vedānta offer an alternative—and equally persuasive—narrative.

Advaita Vedānta, which grew out of the early Upaniṣads and was systematized between the sixth and eighth centuries CE—chiefly by Gaudapāda (fl. early sixth century) and Ādi Śaṅkara (ca. 700–750 CE)—collapses the ordinary subject–object divide by asserting the identity of the individual self, *ātman* (Sanskrit: "breath," "essence," "soul"), with the universal ground of being, *brahman* (Sanskrit: "ultimate reality") (Sharma 2000). This non-dual perspective bridges empirical observation and transcendent insight, inviting us to pursue knowledge as an integrated journey. Beyond Advaita Vedānta, Indian philosophy encompasses a range of streams that celebrate the multiplicity of truth, tracing their roots across different regions and eras of the Indian subcontinent. For example, the Nyāya school—originating in northern India with foundational texts composed between the 2nd century BCE and the 2nd century CE—emphasizes rigorous logical analysis (both deductive and inductive) to dispel error and thereby make *mokṣa* (Sanskrit: "liberation") possible (Matilal 1998). The Yoga tradition, whose early ideas appear in the ancient Vedic texts and was later codified by Patanjali around the 2nd to 4th century CE, demonstrates how integrative practices of meditation, physical discipline, and introspection develop inner awareness and holistic understanding (Bryant 2009). These traditions convey that understanding emerges not solely from distinct logical arguments or isolated mystical experiences, but from an interplay of both. Whether through rigorous analysis, reflective introspection, or mindful living, these philosophies demonstrate that our understanding of reality expands when we engage with its full complexity, avoiding the pitfalls of oversimplification.

This subtle framework encourages us to rethink how we define and value knowledge. It moves us away from compartmentalized, one-dimensional models toward a holistic view that honors both the tangible and the spiritual. In doing so, Indian philosophical traditions offer enduring insights with profound implications for dialogue, education, and societal growth, prompting us to see knowledge as a journey of unity through diversity.

7.3 Bridging the Gaps: Comparative and Integrative Insights

In our increasingly interconnected world—where multifaceted challenges such as climate change, global pandemics, digital privacy crises, and escalating economic inequalities reveal the limitations of singular approaches—a pluralistic perspective on knowledge is not only an academic ideal but also a practical blueprint for resolving these complex modern dilemmas. While traditional discourse has been dominated by the dualism of Western analytical reasoning and Buddhist introspection, the various epistemologies discussed above offer distinct lenses that, when combined, deepen our collective understanding.

Each epistemology—be it *ubuntu*, Indigenous, Islamic, or Indian—contests the notion that knowledge must be confined to isolated, rigid domains. *Ubuntu*, for instance, reframes knowing as a communal endeavor where identity and wisdom are nurtured through shared experience. Indigenous traditions dissolve the boundary between observer and observed, enlivening landscapes with spirit and import. In parallel, Islamic intellectual traditions demonstrate that reason and revelation can effectively coexist, while Indian philosophies celebrate the union of different paths to truth. These individual approaches are not isolated ideals; each contributes vital insights into how communal interrelations, narrative continuity, and a fusion of the empirical with the spiritual can redefine our conception of knowledge.

Considering the communal wisdom of *ubuntu* and the deep, narrative-driven connections of Indigenous traditions, for example, we see that each epistemological approach offers a unique building block for a more comprehensive understanding of reality. The dynamic interplay of rationality and spiritual insight found in Islamic thought, coupled with the non-dual perspectives of Indian philosophy, further reinforces that the divisions between empirical inquiry and lived experience are artificial. This realization invites a cognitive design that honors the strengths of each epistemological approach—transforming fragmentation into a dialogue that is as adaptive as it is inclusive.

Critics might contend that blending such varied approaches risks compromising the rigor of empirical inquiry, with effects on methodological consistency, bias, and reproducibility (Denzin and Lincoln 2018). However, by embedding our analysis within culturally resonant narratives, we preserve empirical rigor while deepening our insights. This synthesis enables a more comprehensive dialogue that bridges individual and collective knowledge alongside rational and spiritual dimensions.

By addressing these epistemological divides, we establish a foundation for transformative educational practices and informed policymaking. Educators and policymakers who draw upon this integrated knowledge can design curricula and strategies that resonate with a heterogenous, global society. Embracing pluralism thus becomes a way to dismantle entrenched silos, stimulate innovative research methodologies, and foster public discourse that is both inclusive and dynamic.

In sum, an integrative perspective can transform our view of knowledge—not as a fixed repository of facts but as an evolving, collective pursuit. By continuously engaging with the unique contributions of *ubuntu*, Indigenous, Islamic, and Indian epistemologies, we can unlock the potential for fruitful dialogue and innovative solutions that mirror the complexity and vibrancy of the world we inhabit.

7.4 Implications for Contemporary Scholarship and Practice

A pluralistic approach to knowledge holds revolutionary potential for education. Crucially, students can begin encountering multiple ways of knowing in the earliest grades, well before they ever set foot on a college campus. By integrating diverse epistemologies—from African communal wisdom and Indigenous storytelling to Islamic synthesis and Indian pluralism—educators can create curricula that reflect a richer, more comprehensive understanding of how we learn. Academic institutions might redesign their learning pathways to incorporate Indigenous knowledge systems alongside Western scientific methods, encouraging students to draw upon both empirical and culturally rooted perspectives. In colleges, this shift would not only deepen scholarly inquiry but also stimulate innovative research methodologies—such as establishing interdisciplinary research teams that pursue culturally grounded inquiry—to reconcile traditional divides. Overall, the result would be an educational experience that honors interconnectedness and prepares students to navigate and contribute to an increasingly complex world.

These far-reaching epistemological perspectives also have real-world implications for policymaking and community engagement. When different ways of knowing inform research and decision-making, policies become more inclusive and better aligned with the needs of varied communities (Smith 2012). This integrated framework would deconstruct rigid silos in public policy, fostering dialogue that brings together empirical evidence and lived experience. In practice, governments and community organizations might launch collaborative initiatives that leverage such integrative approaches, leading to solutions that address social inequalities and promote sustainable development (UNESCO 2021).

Moreover, embracing a pluralistic view of knowledge would nourish cultural life. By reframing binary thinking that separates the rational from the spiritual and the individual from the collective, we enable deeper cultural understanding and creative expression. This synthesis would not only revitalize academic debates but also inspire artists, community leaders, and innovators to rethink tradition, modernity, and the spaces where they intersect.

In essence, these integrative insights would pave the way for more connected responses that meet the demands of our multicultural and rapidly changing global society. By implementing concrete reforms such as curriculum redesign and the formation of interdisciplinary research teams, we can begin to transform theoretical discussions into practical actions that reshape education, dialogue, and public policy for the better.

7.5 Conclusion: Rethinking the Boundaries of Knowledge

While Western analytical reasoning and Buddhist introspection have long dominated our academic discourse, the alternative perspectives presented in this précis reveal fresh, multifaceted ways of understanding the world. They remind us that the quest for knowledge thrives on diversity, context, and the continual interplay between empirical inquiry, lived experience, and natural world of which we are part.

This exploration challenges us to question our assumptions: What do we consider valid knowledge? What role does cultural context play in shaping our definitions of knowledge? How might integrating marginalized epistemologies redress power imbalances in whose knowledge is valued? How might embracing a plurality of epistemologies transform our educational systems, policymaking, and cultural expression? How can embracing a wider spectrum of epistemological traditions transform our approaches to education and public policy? In what ways could blending empirical inquiry with lived experience inspire innovative solutions to global challenges? What mechanisms might expedite the inclusion of pluralistic knowledge systems in mainstream academic discourse? These open-ended questions—and the host of further inquiries they may inspire—welcome ongoing reflection and interdisciplinary dialogue, urging scholars, practitioners, and communities alike to forge new paths in thought and action.

Broadening our perspective enriches intellectual discourse and empowers us to cultivate a future that embraces diversity and fosters adaptability. In this moment of reflection, we are left with a call to curiosity—an invitation to interrogate hidden assumptions, question binaries, embrace the tensions between opposites, explore the spaces where dissimilar traditions of knowing converge, and celebrate the versatility of human insight.

References

Bryant E (2009) The Yoga Sūtras of Patañjali. North Point Press

Cajete G (1994) Look to the mountain: an ecology of indigenous education. University of Arizona Press

Cajete G (2000) Native science: natural laws of interdependence. Clear Light

Deloria V (1999) Spirit and reason. Fulcrum

Denzin N, Lincoln Y (2018) The SAGE handbook of qualitative research. 5th edn. SAGE

Deutsch E (1969) Advaita Vedānta: a philosophical reconstruction. University of Hawaii Press

Gudynas E (2011) Buen vivir: today's tomorrow. Dev 54(4):441–447

Gyekye K (1997) Tradition and modernity: philosophical reflections on the African experience. Oxford University Press

Hanh TN (1975) The miracle of mindfulness. Beacon Press

Hoover J (2007) Ibn Taymiyya's theodicy of perpetual optimism. Brill

Matilal B (1998) The character of logic in India. SUNY Press

Mbiti J (1969) African religions and philosophy. Heinemann

Nasr S (1964) An introduction to Islamic cosmological doctrines. Harvard University Press

Nasr S (1975) Islamic science: an illustrated study. World of Islam Festival Publishing

Ramose M (1999) African philosophy through Ubuntu. Mond Books

Russell B (1945) A history of Western philosophy. Simon & Schuster

Serrat O (2017a) Knowledge as culture. In: Knowledge solutions: tools, methods, and approaches to drive organizational performance, Springer, pp 523–557

Serrat O (2017b) Understanding and developing emotional intelligence. In: Knowledge solutions: tools, methods, and approaches to drive organizational performance, Springer, pp 329–339

Serrat O (2017c) Storytelling. In: Knowledge solutions: tools, methods, and approaches to drive organizational performance, Springer, pp 839–842

Serrat O (2024a) Knowing that and knowing how: must it be either/or? Unpublished manuscript, Georgetown University. https://www.researchgate.net/publication/379514661_Knowing_That_and_Knowing_How_Must_It_Be_EitherOr

Serrat O (2024b) Bridging worlds: Comparative epistemology and the mind–body debate. Unpublished manuscript, Georgetown University. https://www.research gate.net/publication/380611280_Bridging_Worlds_Comparative_Epistemology_and_the_Mind-Body_Problem

Sharma C (2000) Advaita tradition in Indian philosophy. Motilal Banarsidass

Shore B (1982) Sala'ilua: a Samoan mystery. Columbia University Press

Smith L (2012) Decolonizing methodologies: research and indigenous peoples. 2nd edn. Zed Books

Stanner W (1979) White man got no dreaming. Australian National University Press

Tutu D (1999) No future without forgiveness. Doubleday

UNESCO (2021) Reimagining our futures together: a new social contract for education. UNESCO Publishing

Part III

Literary Phenomenology & Cultural Contexts: Exploring Identity, Truth, & Ecology

8

Caring for Our Common Home: Ecocritical Perspectives on Pope Francis's *Laudato Si'*

In a papacy marked by historic milestones, Pope Francis was a pivotal voice in the global fight against the ecological devastation being wrought on the Earth. His groundbreaking encyclical letter, *Laudato Si'* (Francis 2015), presses for a profound ecological conversion, urging humanity to take responsibility for the planet's health and emphasizing the moral imperative to protect "our common home" (Francis 2015, para. 1). The pastoral letter is distinguished by its exceptional global reach and influence, its incorporation of scientific findings, and its holistic approach that uniquely addresses the interconnectedness of cultural, economic, environmental, and social issues. This précis[1] provides an ecocritical analysis of *Laudato Si'*, highlighting its significance in contemporary environmental discourse. Ultimately, the pontifical document serves as both a call to action and a guiding light for sustainable practices worldwide.

8.1 The Roman Catholic Church's Green Revolution

The Roman Catholic Church's stance on ecological concerns has evolved significantly over time (United States Conference of Catholic Bishops 2001). Traditionally, its teachings focused on the stewardship of creation, underscoring

---

[1] Previously published in Serrat, O. (2025). *Anthropogenic solutions for climate change: Achieving environmental peace.* Singapore: Springer.

O. Serrat, *Myth, Philosophy, and Literature*,
https://doi.org/10.1007/978-981-95-2897-4_8

humanity's responsibility to care for the Earth as God's creation. This perspective is rooted in biblical texts, such as the Book of Genesis, which describes humanity's role in tending to the Garden of Eden.

In recent decades, the Church has acknowledged the pressing need to reduce environmental degradation. This shift demonstrates the Church's ability to adapt and respond to global challenges. In 1979, Pope John Paul II (1920–2005) proclaimed Saint Francis of Assisi (1181/82–1226), an Italian mystic, poet, and Catholic friar who founded the Franciscan Order, the heavenly patron of those who promote ecology. Saint Francis was celebrated for his connection with nature and his intense respect for all creation, often referring to the sun and moon as "brother" and "sister" (Britannica 2024). Notably, in the *Common Declaration on Environmental Ethics* (John II and Bartholomew I 2002), Pope John Paul II placed an accent on the moral dimensions of ecological concerns, calling for a global ecological conversion, or change of heart. Pope Benedict XVI (1927–2022), often referred to as the "Green Pope," underlined the importance of environmental stewardship and sustainable development in his encyclical *Caritas in Veritate* (Benedict XVI 2009) and his 2010 World Day of Peace message, *If You Want to Cultivate Peace, Protect Creation* (Benedict XVI 2010).

Born Jorge Mario Bergoglio on December 17, 1936, in Buenos Aires, Argentina, to Italian immigrant parents, Pope Francis was the 266th Pope of the Church. He was ordained a priest in the Society of Jesus in 1969 and became a bishop in 1992. In 1998, he was appointed Archbishop of Buenos Aires and was named a cardinal in 2001 (Francis and Ivereigh 2020). Elected Bishop of Rome on March 13, 2013, he was the first Jesuit pope, the first pope from the Americas, and the first non-European pope in over a millennium. Tellingly, Pope Francis chose his papal name in honor of Saint Francis of Assisi.

Under the new pontiff, the Church intensified its advocacy for environmental stewardship and sustainable development, urging comprehensive and urgent action for environmental protection. This advocacy confronts critical issues such as climate change, deforestation, desertification, habitat destruction, loss of biodiversity, invasive species, ocean acidification, overfishing, plastic waste, pollution, resource depletion, and soil degradation. Shortly after his election, Pope Francis initiated the preparation of *Laudato Si'*. He enlisted climate and environmental science experts to gather the most accurate data on the state of the planet. He then invited theologians to engage with this data in a global dialogue with experts. Theologians and scientists collaborated until they reached a synthesis. *Laudato Si'* firmly positioned ecology as a central theme in Church discourse (Deane-Drummond 2017).

Strategically timed for publication just before the 2015 United Nations Climate Change Conference (COP21) in Paris, many attribute the historic undertaking of the so-called Paris Agreement (United Nations 2015) to the influence of this work and the efforts of Pope Francis. The Paris Agreement aspires to keep the global temperature rise this century well below 2°C above pre-industrial levels and pursue efforts to limit the increase to 1.5°C.

The pontiff aimed for *Laudato Si'* to reach a worldwide audience and spark international discussion. The Church remains one of the largest religious institutions globally, with a substantial presence in various countries and cultures. Its reach and influence can mobilize millions of people towards sustainable practices and policies. Currently, there are approximately 1.4 billion baptized Catholics worldwide, reflecting a slight rise from previous years, with notable growth in Africa and Asia (Quiñones 2024). Besides, while secular societies may not adhere to religious doctrines, the ethical and moral arguments presented by religious leaders can still engage a large audience.

8.2 *Laudato Si'*: A Call for Ecological Conversion

"All it takes is one good person to restore hope!" Pope Francis exclaimed in *Laudato Si'* (Francis 2015, para. 71). During the pontiff's papacy, the world faced significant challenges, including pandemics; rising economic inequalities; political polarization; migration and refugee crises; religious persecution and violence in various parts of the world (e.g., China, India, Middle East, Myanmar, Nigeria, Pakistan); technological advancements and ethical concerns; and conflicts in Syria (2011–), Yemen (2014–), Myanmar (2021–), Ukraine (2022–), and Israel-Palestine (2023–). These challenges shaped Pope Francis's papacy and his efforts to address them through advocacy, dialogue, and pastoral care. Moreover, the urgent necessity for climate action has never been more critical. Understandably, the pope's tenure was marked by a strong accent on social justice, advocacy for the marginalized, and environmental stewardship, reflecting his commitment to tackling these critical global issues.

In *Laudato Si'*, Pope Francis reflected on the world's ecological concerns and did not mince words: "Due to an ill-considered exploitation of nature, humanity runs the risk of destroying it and becoming in turn a victim of this degradation" (Francis 2015, para. 4). "Every effort to protect and improve our world entails substantial changes in lifestyles, models of production and consumption, and the established structures of power which today govern societies" (Francis 2015, para. 5). "The [E]arth, our home, is beginning to look more and more like an immense pile of filth" (Francis 2015, para. 21). "[N]owadays we must forcefully reject the notion that our being created in God's image and given dominion over the [E]arth justifies absolute domination over other creatures" (Francis 2015, para. 67). "A global consensus is essential for confronting the deeper problems, which cannot be resolved by unilateral actions on the part of individual countries" (Francis 2015, para. 164). As the first papal letter devoted to environmentalism, *Laudato Si'* urges readers to fundamentally reconsider our relationship with the planet. Praised by educators, environmentalists, scientists, and leaders of various faiths for its balanced poise, the pastoral letter continues to significantly influence international environmental discourse, shaping the Church's environmental policies and encouraging sustainable practices worldwide (Handley 2016).

In support of its call to action for environmental stewardship and social justice, *Laudato Si'* articulated several key themes:

- **Biodiversity.** The encyclical makes obvious the vital significance of preserving biodiversity and recognizing the intrinsic value of all living creatures.
- **Climate Change.** The encyclical points to the broad scientific agreement on climate change and its catastrophic impacts, especially on the poor and vulnerable.
- **Consumerism and Waste.** The encyclical critiques the pervasive culture of consumerism and the throwaway mentality, advocating for sustainable and responsible consumption patterns.
- **Ethical and Spiritual Dimensions.** The encyclical calls for a deep moral and spiritual renewal, urging individuals and communities to adopt a more respectful and caring attitude towards nature.
- **Global Solidarity.** The encyclical highlights the necessity of global cooperation and solidarity to tackle environmental challenges, stressing the importance of dialogue and collective action.
- **Integral Ecology.** The encyclical points to the interconnectedness of all creation, promoting an approach that integrates environmental, economic, social, and cultural dimensions because "Everything is related" (Francis 2015, para. 92). As stated in the encyclical, the elements of integral ecology that enable us to consider every aspect of the global crisis are environmental, economic, and social ecology; cultural ecology; ecology of daily life; the principle of the common good; and justice between generations.

- **Social justice.** The encyclical links environmental degradation to social injustice, exposing how the poor and vulnerable, including marginalized and indigenous peoples, are disproportionately affected and campaigning for their rights and dignity.
- **Technological and Economic Factors.** The encyclical considers the role of technology and economic systems in environmental degradation, calling for a critical evaluation to ensure they align with sustainable and ethical principles.

Several other religious texts have emphasized environmental stewardship and ethical responsibility. The *Earth Charter*, an international declaration endorsed by various religious groups, recognizes the interconnectedness of all life and the need for sustainable development and social justice (Earth Charter Initiative 2000). Islamic teachings on the unity of creation and the responsibility of humans to act as stewards of the Earth, known as *tawhid*, are rooted in the *Quran* and *Hadith* (Nasr 1996). *The Green Bible* is a special edition of the Bible that highlights scriptures related to environmental stewardship, including essays and a green index to guide readers in understanding the biblical basis for caring for creation (Bible 2008). Ecumenical Patriarch Bartholomew I, often referred to as the "Green Patriarch," has issued numerous encyclicals and statements on the ethical and spiritual dimensions of ecological responsibility (Bartholomew 2003). Hindu texts like the *Bhagavad Gita* and the *Vedas* point out the sanctity of nature and the responsibility of humans to safeguard and maintain the environment (Dwivedi 1993). Similarly, the concept of interdependence and the principle of non-harming (*ahimsa*) in Buddhism encourage a respectful and mindful relationship with the natural world (Kabilsingh 1998). However, *Laudato Si'* stands out for its unparalleled global reach and influence, its integration of scientific findings, and its comprehensive approach that uniquely attends to the interconnectedness of cultural, economic, environmental, and social issues.

Building on the themes of *Laudato Si'*, Pope Francis advocated for urgent action against climate change, lamenting its disproportionate impact on the poor and vulnerable. *Our Mother Earth* (Francis 2020) set forth a Christian vision of ecology, gathered from his writings and discourses. In the exclusive new essay that concludes *Our Mother Earth* (Francis 2020), Pope Francis developed a "theology of ecology" in a most ethical and spiritual discourse. This last chapter shares thoughts on how a Christian vision of care for our common home transcends a purely secular approach to ecology. The pope remarked that humanity's capacity for communion conditions the state of creation, suggesting that it is humanity's destiny to determine the destiny of the universe. This theological perspective underscores the interconnectedness of all creation and seeks a global ecological conversion, urging individuals, communities, and societies to adopt sustainable practices and recognize the moral and ethical dimensions of environmental stewardship. Also in 2020, the pontiff introduced the Laudato Si' Action Platform (https://laudatosiactionplat form.org/), a seven-year initiative promoting sustainability across various sectors. The platform suggests concrete steps and resources for individuals and communities to implement sustainable practices. His apostolic exhortation, *Laudate Deum* (Francis 2023), built on *Laudato Si'*, summoning urgent and coordinated climate action. Pope Francis's environmental advocacy extended to international forums, urging nations to honor the Paris Agreement (United Nations 2015) and mitigate climate change.

8.3   Ecocriticism: Bridging Literature and Environmental Discourse

Ecocriticism is an interdisciplinary field that encourages a deeper appreciation of the natural world and promotes environmental awareness and activism through literary analysis. In the face of escalating environmental crises, ecocriticism has become increasingly significant in contemporary environmental discourse (Bergthaller et al. 2014). By integrating insights from various fields, ecocriticism contributes to a comprehensive understanding of ecological problems and solutions (Glotfelty and Fromm 1996). Specifically, it observes how literature portrays nature, environmental issues, and human interactions with the natural world. Narratives shape societal values and behaviors; by analyzing texts, ecocritics seek to understand how literature reflects, critiques, or influences environmental attitudes and policies.

As environmental crises grow more urgent, ecocriticism has gained significant traction in contemporary environmental discourse (Garrard 2014). Garrard (2023) identified six overarching political and philosophical frames that understand environmental crises in their own way: cornucopia, ecofeminism, ecological modernization, new materialism, political ecology and environmental justice, and radical ecology. Key concepts reflecting the diversity within ecocriticism include animals, the Earth, indigeneity, pastoral, pollution, and wilderness (Garrard 2023). A central tenet of ecocriticism is the recognition of the interconnectedness between humans and the environment. This perspective challenges the traditional anthropocentric view that places humans at the center of the universe, advocating instead for a more rounded understanding of the world (Glotfelty and Fromm 1996).

Pastoral poets who foreshadowed contemporary eco-activism include William Wordsworth (1770–1850), Gerard Manley Hopkins (1844–1889), and G. K. Chesterton (1874–1936) (Bate 1991). Notable early works of fiction and non-fiction in the genres of nature writing and transcendentalism, as well as environmental science and advocacy, include *Walden; or, Life in the Woods* (Thoreau 1854) and *Silent Spring* (Carson 1962). In contemporary environmental discourse, works of fiction, non-fiction, and poetry that treat themes such as climate change, deforestation, and pollution serve as powerful tools for environmental advocacy. By engaging readers emotionally and intellectually, these texts foster a deeper connection to the natural world and a greater sense of responsibility for its preservation (Buell 2005).

Moreover, ecocriticism underscores the importance of diverse perspectives in understanding environmental issues. It recognizes that different cultures and communities have unique relationships with the environment, shaped by stheir histories, traditions, and values. By examining a wide range of literary works from various cultural contexts, ecocritics uncover alternative ways of thinking about and relating to nature. An inclusive approach is necessary to deal with contemporary environmental challenges, as it fosters cross-cultural dialogue and collaboration (Clark 2011).

Another significant aspect of ecocriticism is its focus on the ethical implications of environmental issues. It asserts the moral responsibilities of individuals, societies, and governments in preventing environmental crises. By analyzing how literature portrays the consequences of environmental degradation, ecocritics shed light on the ethical dilemmas and injustices associated with these issues. For example, many literary works draw attention to the disproportionate impact of environmental problems on marginalized communities, highlighting the need for environmental justice (Rueckert 1978).

In addition to its contributions to literary studies, ecocriticism has influenced other disciplines, such as philosophy, political science, and sociology. Its interdisciplinary nature allows for a more comprehensive understanding of environmental issues, integrating varied insights into complex ecological problems. This approach remains particularly relevant in contemporary environmental discourse, where the interconnectedness of ecological, economic, and social systems is increasingly recognized (Garrard 2014; Heise 2008).

Furthermore, ecocriticism has stimulated new forms of creative expression that engage with environmental themes. Eco-documentaries, eco-fiction, eco-films, eco-photography, eco-poetry, and environmental memoirs are just a few examples of genres that have emerged in response to the growing awareness of ecological issues (Bryson 2002; Dwyer 2010; Kimmerer 2013; Parini 1999; Schneider-Mayerson 2018; Williams 2017). These works not only contribute to the literary landscape but also serve as important cultural artifacts that reflect and shape our collective understanding of the environment (Glotfelty and Fromm 1996).

8.4   *Laudato Si'* Through the Lens of Ecocriticism

Key themes of ecocriticism that are particularly relevant to *Laudato Si'* are:

- **Critique of Technocratic and Industrial Paradigms.** Ecocriticism critiques the dominance of technocratic and industrial paradigms that prioritize economic growth over environmental sustainability. The Vatican directive challenged the technocratic and industrial mindset and promoted a more sustainable and ethical approach to development.
- **Cultural Dimensions.** Ecocriticism appraises the cultural dimensions of human–nature relationships. The Vatican directive appreciated the spiritual significance of nature and sponsored a cultural shift towards greater environmental awareness and stewardship.
- **Environmental Justice.** Ecocriticism often brings up issues of environmental justice, focusing on how environmental degradation disproportionately affects marginalized communities. The Vatican directive urged social justice and equitable distribution of resources, reasoning there was a moral imperative to protect the poor and vulnerable.
- **Ethical Responsibility.** Ecocriticism promotes the idea of ethical responsibility towards the environment. The Vatican directive called for a global ecological conversion, urging individuals, communities, and societies to adopt sustainable lifestyles and practices.
- **Integration of Science and Humanities.** Ecocriticism often integrates scientific knowledge with literary and cultural analysis to illuminate environmental issues. The Vatican directive incorporated scientific evidence on climate change and environmental degradation in favor of an interdisciplinary approach to solving ecological problems.

- **Interconnectedness.** Ecocriticism grasps the interconnectedness of all living beings and the environment. The Vatican directive clarified that environmental, social, economic, and political issues were deeply intertwined and stressed the need for a holistic approach to environmental issues.

These themes illustrate how *Laudato Si'* aligned with and contributed to the broader discourse of ecocriticism, offering a comprehensive and ethically grounded perspective on environmental issues. In addition, *Laudato Si'* drew attention to:

- **Consumerism.** The apostolic letter considered the culture of consumerism and irresponsible development and recommended sustainable practices and a shift towards simpler, more mindful living.
- **Dialogue and Solidarity.** The apostolic letter encouraged dialogue and solidarity, promoting collaboration among scientists, policymakers, religious leaders, and all sectors of society to develop practical solutions to environmental challenges.
- **Ecological Conversion.** The apostolic letter pressed for a transformation in how humanity views and interacts with the environment, urging everyone to take responsibility for the planet's health.
- **Ethics and Spirituality.** The apostolic letter framed environmental stewardship as a core component of the Christian faith, reiterating the moral imperative to protect our common home.
- **Impact on the Poor.** The apostolic letter pointed out the disproportionate impact of environmental degradation on the poor and vulnerable, calling for environmental justice and equitable solutions.
- **Integral Ecology.** The apostolic letter introduced the concept of integral ecology, promoting a holistic approach to environmental crises because ecology encompasses far more than just the care of nature.

Laudato Si' was a comprehensive document that took up many key themes of ecocriticism. However, there are a few themes, some of which were brought to light by Garrard (2023), that were not as prominently featured or were approached differently:

- **Animal Studies.** Animal studies scrutinize the ethical considerations of human–animal relationships and the treatment of animals. While the pontifical document acknowledged the importance of caring for all creatures, it did not thoroughly appraise the ethical dimensions of human–animal relationships.

- **Apocalypse.** Apocalyptic ecocriticism often critiques apocalyptic narratives and sponsors proactive environmental stewardship over fatalistic outlooks. Similarly, the pontifical document aimed to inspire hope and action for environmental stewardship, promoting global dialogue and collective effort rather than yielding to apocalyptic fears or indifference.
- **Deep Ecology.** Deep ecology champions a shift in human consciousness, recognizing the intrinsic value of all living beings beyond their utility to humans. While the pontifical document highlighted the interconnectedness of all life and the need for a holistic approach, it primarily focused on the ethical and moral responsibilities of humans rather than advocating for a radical shift in consciousness.
- **Ecofeminism.** Ecofeminism examines the links between the exploitation of women and the environment, arguing that both are rooted in patriarchal structures. While the pontifical document strongly advocated for social justice and gender equality, it did not explicitly frame these issues within the context of ecofeminism.
- **Postcolonial Ecocriticism.** Postcolonial ecocriticism looks into the intersections of environmental issues and colonial histories, focusing on how colonialism has impacted both the environment and the poor and vulnerable. While the pontifical document explicitly rebuked the exploitation of the poor and vulnerable, it did not delve into the specific historical and ongoing impacts of colonialism on the environment.
- **Urban Ecocriticism.** Urban ecocriticism analyzes the relationship between urban environments and ecological issues, focusing on how cities can be designed and managed to be more sustainable. The pontifical document discussed the importance of sustainable development and the need for ecological conversion, but it did not specifically touch on the particular concerns of urban ecocriticism.

These themes highlight areas where *Laudato Si'* could have focused its discussion to align more closely with the conventional discourse of ecocriticism, if such a need had arisen. Notwithstanding, the encyclical remains a most significant and influential document that, with remarkable brevity, attended to many critical environmental and social issues in under 180 concise pages (246 paragraphs).

8.5 Intersections of Faith and Philosophy: *Laudato Si'* and Morton's Ecological Thought

Timothy Morton is a contemporary philosopher and ecocritic known for his work on ecology, literature, and object-oriented ontology, a new school of thought in metaphysics that explores the existence and agency of non-human objects. Object-oriented ontology challenges the traditional privileging of human existence over non-human entities and posits that objects exist independently of human perception and interaction. Consequently, it rejects the idea that human existence should prevail over the existence of nonhuman objects. Morton has authored numerous books, including *The Ecological Thought* (Morton 2010), *Hyperobjects: Philosophy and Ecology after the End of the World* (Morton 2013), and *Dark Ecology: For a Logic of Future Coexistence* (Morton 2016). His work often probes the intersections of ecological studies and object-oriented thought, advocating for a radical rethinking of human relationships with non-human entities and the environment.

Embarking on a journey through *Laudato Si'* with the insights of Morton (2010) is akin to opening a dialogue between two discerning perspectives on our relationship with the environment. Morton (2010) dismantles the illusion of nature as a distant, untouched realm, urging us to see the interconnected web of life that includes the artificial and the synthetic. *Laudato Si'*, on the other hand, advocated for an integral ecology that weaves together the cultural, economic, environmental, and social threads of our existence. In distinct ways but with the same intention, these works invite us to reconsider our place in the world and embrace a holistic approach to environmental stewardship.

Despite their different origins—one rooted in religious doctrine and the other in environmental philosophy—*Laudato Si'* and Morton (2010) showed up the urgent need for a shift in how humanity perceives and interacts with the environment. These works converged on the idea of interconnectedness:

* **Critique of Consumerism and Technological Impact.** Both Morton (2010) and *Laudato Si'* critiqued the prevailing culture of consumerism and the detrimental impact of technology on the environment. "Modern economic structures have drastically affected the environment" (Morton 2010, p. 4). "Do we have to go into outer space to care for Earth? Do we need high technology? Do we need Google Earth to imagine Earth? Is

Western science and power the only path to ecological awareness?" (Morton 2010, p. 25). Similarly, *Laudato Si'* critiqued the throwaway culture and the unsustainable consumption patterns that contribute to environmental degradation (Handley 2016). "[W]e cannot fail to consider the effects of environmental deterioration, current models of development and the throwaway culture on people's lives" (Francis 2015, para. 43). The encyclical invited a critical evaluation of technological advancements and economic practices to ensure they align with sustainable and ethical principles.

- **Ethical and Spiritual Dimensions.** While Morton's (2010) work was grounded in environmental philosophy, *Laudato Si'* incorporated strong ethical and spiritual dimensions. "Cultural limitations in different eras often affected the perception of [...] ethical and spiritual treasures, yet by constantly returning to their sources, religions will be better equipped to respond to today's needs" (Francis 2015, para. 200). The encyclical encouraged a spiritual awakening and a moral response to the ecological crisis, urging individuals and communities to adopt a more respectful and caring attitude towards nature (Handley 2016). Morton's (2010) ecological thought, though not explicitly spiritual, also implied an ethical responsibility towards the environment, emphasizing the need for a shift in how we think about and engage with the world around us. "The ecological thought must imagine economic change: otherwise it's just another piece on the board game of capitalist ideology?" (Morton 2010, p. 19).

- **Global Solidarity and Collective Action.** Morton (2010) and *Laudato Si'* ascribed much importance to global solidarity and collective action in the face of environmental challenges. *Laudato Si'* encouraged global cooperation and dialogue to tackle environmental issues, stressing the need for a unified response (Iheka 2017). "We require a new and universal solidarity" (Francis 2015, para. 14). Morton (2010), too, highlights the necessity of thinking beyond localism and embracing a global perspective on ecological interconnectedness. "If we think the ecological thought, two things happen. Our perspective becomes very vast. More and more aspects of the Universe become included in the ecological thought. At the same time, our view becomes very profound" (Morton 2010, p. 38). Morton (2010) and *Laudato Si'* recognized that addressing the ecological crisis requires a concerted effort from all sectors of society. "Perhaps the sentiment we're going for is not 'We can because we must,' but rather 'We must because we are'" (Morton 2010, p. 124).

- **Interconnectedness and Integral Ecology.** At the heart of both Morton (2010) and *Laudato Si'* was the concept of interconnectedness. Morton (2010) challenged the notion of nature as a separate, pristine entity, arguing instead for an ecological thought that acknowledges the entanglement of all life forms, including the synthetic and the artificial. "The ecological thought imagines interconnectedness, which I call the mesh. Who or what is interconnected with what or with whom? The mesh of interconnected things is vast, perhaps immeasurably so. Each entity in the mesh looks strange. Nothing exists all by itself, and so nothing is fully 'itself.' There is curiously 'less' of the Universe at the same time, and for the same reasons, as we see 'more' of it." (Morton 2010, p. 15). Morton (2010) argued that all forms of life are entangled in a vast, intricate mesh, where no being or object exists independently from the ecological web. This idea resonates with *Laudato Si's* concept of integral ecology (Handley 2016; Iheka 2017). "To seek only a technical remedy to each environmental problem which comes up is to separate what is in reality interconnected and to mask the true and deepest problems of the global system" (Francis 2015, para. 111). Comparably, Morton (2010) and *Laudato Si'* advocated for a comprehensive understanding of ecology that transcends traditional boundaries and recognizes the interdependence of all life forms.

Morton (2010) and *Laudato Si'* offered complementary perspectives on the ecological crisis. While Morton's (2010) work provided a philosophical framework for understanding ecological interconnectedness, *Laudato Si'* integrated this understanding with a call for ethical and spiritual transformation. In unison, Morton (2010) and *Laudato Si'* underscored the urgent need for a holistic approach to environmental stewardship, one that recognizes the interconnectedness of all life and the moral imperative to protect our common home.

Laudato Si' drew on a wide range of sources, including previous papal teachings, scientific research, and theological reflections. While Morton (2010) is noteworthy in the field of ecocriticism and shares some thematic similarities with *Laudato Si'*, such as the interconnectedness of all life and the critique of anthropocentrism, there is no direct evidence to suggest that Morton (2010) specifically influenced the apostolic letter.

8.6 *Laudato Si'*: A Catalyst for Ecological Transformation

Laudato Si' demonstrated that religious leaders can play a crucial role in environmental discourse by leveraging their moral authority and social influence to shift attitudes and behaviors, foster a sense of stewardship among their followers, and inspire action. This aligns with theories of moral authority and social influence. Their unique position enables them to bridge the gap between scientific understanding and ethical imperatives, making complex environmental issues more accessible and urgent to a broader audience. By framing environmental care as an ethical and spiritual duty, religious leaders can galvanize their followers to adopt more sustainable practices and advocate for policies that protect the planet.

Laudato Si' was a landmark document in the realm of environmental advocacy. It highlighted the interconnectedness of all creation and the moral imperative to care for our common home. By framing environmental issues through the lens of Catholic social teaching, Pope Francis enriched the conversation to include ethical and spiritual dimensions, making it clear that environmental degradation was not just a scientific or economic issue, but a moral crisis. He challenged humankind to rethink its relationship with nature and adopt more sustainable lifestyles.

Laudato Si' set a precedent for future environmental advocacy by stressing the importance of integrating ethical and spiritual perspectives into the discourse. It encouraged other religious leaders and institutions to take a more active role in promoting environmental stewardship. The encyclical also stressed the need for global cooperation and solidarity, suggesting that effective environmental action requires a collective effort that transcends national and cultural boundaries. This approach can hearten a more inclusive and comprehensive strategy for combating environmental challenges. Potential areas for further research include:

- **Case Studies of Successful Religious Environmental Movements.** Document and analyze successful environmental movements led by religious groups, identifying key factors that contributed to their success and lessons that can be applied to other contexts.
- **Ethical Frameworks for Environmental Decision-Making.** Develop and analyze ethical frameworks that incorporate religious principles to guide environmental decision-making and policy development.

- **Impact of Religious Teachings on Environmental Behavior.** Study the influence of religious teachings on the environmental attitudes and behaviors of adherents, identifying effective strategies for promoting sustainable practices within faith communities.
- **Interfaith Environmental Initiatives.** Investigate how different religious traditions can collaborate on environmental projects and advocacy, fostering a united front for ecological sustainability.
- **Role of Religious Institutions in Policy Advocacy.** Reflect on how religious institutions can engage in policy advocacy at local, national, and international levels to support environmental initiatives.

These areas of research can offer valuable insights into the intersection of religion and environmentalism, helping to shape more inclusive approaches to the ecological crisis. "Start by doing what is necessary, then what is possible, and suddenly you are doing the impossible," Saint Francis of Assisi (n.d.) is famously quoted as saying. One might reasonably assume that Pope Francis was in full agreement.

8.7 *Laudato Si'*: Sparking New Directions in Ecocritical Research

Laudato Si' has significant implications for ecocriticism. Here are some key points:

- **Call for Ecological Conversion.** The concept of "ecological conversion" in the pastoral letter insisted on a transformation in how humans relate to nature. This idea can motivate ecocritics to weigh up themes of transformation and renewal in environmental literature.
- **Critique of Technocratic Paradigms.** The pastoral letter challenged the technocratic paradigm that prioritizes technological and economic growth over environmental sustainability. This critique resonates with ecocritical analyses that challenge dominant narratives of progress and development.
- **Holistic Approach to Environmental Issues.** The pastoral letter advocated for a holistic approach to environmental problems, considering social, economic, and cultural factors. This aligns with ecocriticism's interdisciplinary nature, encouraging scholars to explore the interconnectedness of various aspects of human life and the environment.

- **Integration of Ethical and Spiritual Dimensions.** The pastoral letter brought a moral and spiritual perspective to environmental issues, underlining the ethical responsibility of humans to care for the Earth. This enriches ecocriticism by adding a layer of ethical and spiritual analysis to environmental literature.
- **Promotion of Global Solidarity.** The pastoral letter drove home the need for global cooperation and solidarity to address environmental challenges. This perspective can embolden ecocritics to consider global and cross-cultural dimensions in their analyses.

These implications underscore the potential of *Laudato Si'* to enrich and expand ecocriticism. By offering new research avenues, the encyclical addressed Buell's (2005) challenge for the discipline to establish its significance beyond academia.

8.8   *Ad Astra per Aspera*

This précis deliberated several themes, starting with the Church's intensified focus on environmental ethics, highlighted by Pope Francis's momentous encyclical, *Laudato Si'*. It then transitioned to ecocriticism, analyzing how the central themes of this interdisciplinary field were reflected in the Vatican directive. Next, by focusing on a specific work of ecocriticism, the précis examined the intersections of faith and philosophy as seen in *Laudato Si'* and Morton (2010). Great works inherently provide ample food for thought. Consequently, the précis also considered how *Laudato Si'* might serve as a catalyst for further religious environmental movements and posited that it could enhance and enlarge the field of ecocriticism itself.

In the prologue to *Let Us Dream: The Path to a Better Future* (Francis and Ivereigh 2020), the pontiff reflected on a line in Friedrich Hölderlin's hymn, *Patmos*: "But where the danger is, also grows the saving power" (cited in Francis and Ivereigh 2020, p. 6), meaning that even in the midst of crisis, there is always a way to escape destruction. In *Laudato Si'*, Pope Francis echoed this sentiment, offering a beacon of hope and a call to action for humanity. "Humanity still has the ability to work together in building our common home" (Francis 2015, para. 13). Pope Francis described *Laudato Si'* as a social encyclical, explaining that "[t]he green and the social go hand in hand" (Francis and Ivereigh 2020, p. 32).

In the final chapters of *Laudato Si'*, Pope Francis outlined transformative pathways for dialogue and action to break free from the cycle of self-destruction that threatens our world. These pathways include: fostering international economic dialogue on environmental issues; crafting innovative national and local policies; ensuring transparency in decision-making processes; harmonizing politics and economy for human well-being; and bridging the gap between religions and science (Francis 2015, paras. 163–201; Serrat 2024a, 2024b, 2024c, 2024d). Pope Francis also championed ecological education and spirituality "to enable the development of new convictions, attitudes, and forms of life" (Francis 2015, para. 202).

8.9 Epilogue

Sight-Worn

Sight-worn lidless eyes turning inward
Seek darkness in the past,
Lie me in a shaded recess of the mind
Where kind memories diffuse a softer glow.
I mold words for your ears.
My fingers trace the contours of your thoughts,
A touch ever so light the pattern arches back,
Murmuring worlds, tasting the feel.
A groomed engine then,
We become an instant and breathing must be willed.
It is colder now.
The wire leading your voice through the maze underground chills it hard metallic—
I shall wear a tie for the rest of my life.

In this my Tokyo train (another rush hour day)
The shuttling of matter in entrails to the tune
Of a perched employee orchestrating the boom.
Toranomon. Mutes roam the corridors head bowed,
Trying the step to ground level, and emerge in the rain.
A hundred little gray worlds bloom in a flurry of umbrellas,
Hop graceless o'er puddles and puncture in doorways.
Sowing raincoats, myriads rush to the masque
Donning smiles on the way.

My pen as a lance probes and pokes at the wall till,
Self-propelled and sudden-sucked,
Spinning and swirling through the envelope,

Dizzying free, a part becomes the whole.
I am world, my hair foliage.
A courser wind-swept, my blood is new sap wailing.
A crumpled page.

In this his unbuilt house,
My father shall cajole the jet lag out our bones
And with it cement stones that to the hill shall draw the family in pairs.
Amber-suffused limbs by the green apple fire,
Bristling up down its beams of warmth to keep,
We shall suffer the dark to signal the way home.
The glasses at our hands—chalices rapt in ice—bitter sweetness encompass.
A gentian-flavored drink sings another for the road,
Tomorrow being Monday.

Please leave me not,
Through want of prevenient grace,
To partake with dodoes, dinosaurs, aborigines too,
Of a stuporous fate.
'Fore the last yards of a once endless race,
Run now with the faltering office gait of
I that stitched, pant, and feverish spit more froth in unseeing eyes,
Lord of Life, show me Thy Grace. (Serrat 2023)

References

Bartholomew I (2003) Encyclicals and statements on environmental issues. Ecumenical Patriarchate

Bate J (1991) Romantic ecology: wordsworth and the environmental tradition. Routledge

Benedict XVI (2009) Caritas in Veritate: on integral human development in charity and truth. Vatican Press. https://www.vatican.va/content/benedict-xvi/en/encyclicals/documents/hf_ben-xvi_enc_20090629_caritas-in-veritate.html

Benedict XVI (2010, Jan 1). If you want to cultivate peace, protect creation. https://www.vatican.va/content/benedict-xvi/en/messages/peace/documents/hf_ben-xvi_mes_20091208_xliii-world-day-peace.html

Bergthaller H, Emmett R, Johns-Putra A, Kneitz A, Lidström S, McCorristine S, Pérez Ramos I, Phillips D, Rigby K, Robin L (2014) Mapping Common Ground: ecocriticism, Environmental History, and the Environmental Humanities. Environ Humanit 5(1):261–276

Bible G (2008) The Green Bible. HarperOne

Britannica. (2024). St. Francis of Assisi. https://www.britannica.com/biography/ Saint-Francis-of-Assisi

Bryson JS (Ed.) (2002) Ecopoetry: a critical introduction. University of Utah Press

Buell L (2005) The future of environmental criticism: environmental crisis and literary imagination. Wiley-Blackwell

Carson R (1962) Silent spring. Houghton Mifflin

Clark T (2011) The Cambridge introduction to literature and the environment. Cambridge University Press

Dean-Drummond C (2017) A primer in ecotheology. Cascade Companions

Dwivedi O (1993) Hinduism and ecology. In: Chapple C, Tucker ME (eds) Worldviews and ecology. Orbis Books, pp 193–208

Dwyer J (2010) Where the wild books are: a field guide to ecofiction. University of Nevada Press

Earth Charter Initiative (2000) The Earth charter. Earth Charter Commission

Francis P (2015) Laudato Si': on care for our common home. Vatican Press. https:// www.vatican.va/content/francesco/en/encyclicals/documents/papa-francesco _20150524_enciclica-laudato-si.html

Francis P (2020) Our mother Earth: a Christian reading of the challenge of the environment. Our Sunday Visitor

Francis P (2023) Laudate Deum: on the urgency of climate action. Vatican Press. https://www.vatican.va/content/francesco/en/apost_exhortations/documents/ 20231004-laudate-deum.html

Francis P, Ivereigh A (2020) Let us dream: the path to a better future. Simon & Schuster

Garrard G (2014) The Oxford handbook of ecocriticism. Oxford University Press

Garrard G (2023) Ecocriticism. 3rd edn. Routledge

Glotfelty C, Fromm H (1996) The ecocriticism reader: landmarks in literary ecology. University of Georgia Press

Handley G (2016) *Laudato Si'* and the postsecularism of the environmental humanities. Environ Humanit 8(2):277–284

Heise U (2008) Sense of place and sense of planet: the environmental imagination of the global. Oxford University Press

Iheka C (2017) Pope Francis' integral ecology and environmentalism for the poor. Environ Ethics 39(3):243–259

John PII, BartholomewI (2002) Common declaration on environmental ethics. Vatican Press. https://www.vatican.va/content/john-paul-ii/en/speeches/2002/ june/documents/hf_jp-ii_spe_20020610_venice-declaration.html

Kabilsingh C (1998) Buddhism and ecology: the interconnection of dharma and deeds. Motilal Banarsidass

Kimmerer RW (2013) Braiding sweetgrass: indigenous wisdom, scientific knowledge, and the teachings of plants. Milkweed Editions

Morton T (2010) The ecological thought. Harvard University Press

Morton T (2013) Hyperobjects: philosophy and ecology after the end of the world. University of Minnesota Press

Morton T (2016) Dark ecology: for a logic of future coexistence. Columbia University Press

Nasr SH (1996) Religion and the order of nature. Oxford University Press

Parini J (1999) Poems for a small planet: contemporary American nature poetry. Middlebury College Press

Quiñones K (2024, Apr 8). The Catholic Church by the numbers: more Catholics but fewer vocations. Catholic News Agency. https://www.catholicnewsagency.com/news/257316/the-catholic-church-by-the-numbers-more-catholics-but-fewer-vocations

Rueckert W (1978) Literature and ecology: an experiment in ecocriticism. In Glotfelty C, Fromm H (eds) The ecocriticism reader: landmarks in literary ecology. University of Georgia Press, pp 105–123

Schneider-Mayerson M (2018) The influence of climate fiction: an empirical survey of readers. Environmental Humanities 10(2):473–500

Serrat O (2023) Mere words, these: 32 poems in free verse. Troubador Publishing Ltd

Serrat O (2024a). ICYMI: Climate security rhymes with national security. Unpublished manuscript, Georgetown University. https://www.researchgate.net/publication/378545941_ICYMI_Climate_Security_Rhymes_with_National_Security

Serrat O (2024b). Beggar thy neighbor to beggar thyself: why China and the United States must cooperate to address climate change. Unpublished manuscript, Georgetown University. https://www.researchgate.net/publication/380212272_Beggar_Thy_Neighbor_to_Beggar_Thyself_Why_China_and_the_United_States_Must_Cooperate_to_Address_Climate_Change

Serrat O (2024c). Redefining norms: A modern-day Marshall Plan for climate adaptation and climate justice. Unpublished manuscript, Georgetown University. https://www.researchgate.net/publication/380530326_Redefining_Norms_A_Modern-Day_Marshall_Plan_for_Climate_Adaptation_and_Climate_Justice

Serrat O (2024d). Bridging worlds: Comparative epistemology and the mind–body debate. Unpublished manuscript, Georgetown University. https://www.researchgate.net/publication/380611280_Bridging_Worlds_Comparative_Epistemology_and_the_Mind-Body_Problem

Thoreau H (1854) Walden; or, life in the woods. Ticknor and Fields

United Nations. (2015). Paris Agreement. https://unfccc.int/sites/default/files/english_paris_agreement.pdf

United States Conference of Catholic Bishops. (2001, June 15). Global climate change: A plea for dialogue, prudence, and the common good. https://www.usccb.org/resources/global-climate-change-plea-dialogue-prudence-and-common-good

Williams F (2017) The nature fix: why nature makes us happier, healthier, and more creative. W.W. Norton & Company

9

Exploring Identity: Antonio Muñoz Molina's (2015) Take on *Don Quixote*

9.1 From La Mancha to the World: 400 Years of *Don Quixote*

Imagine a world where a man in rusty armor sets out on a quest to revive chivalry, where the boundaries between reality and fiction blur, and where the power of imagination transforms the mundane into the extraordinary. This is the world of *Don Quixote* (Cervantes 2003), a novel that has captivated readers for centuries. In 2015, people around the world commemorated the 400th anniversary of *Don Quixote* (Cervantes 2003), which many regard as the first modern novel. This significant milestone in literary history was celebrated internationally through vibrant conferences, cultural festivities, film screenings, new editions, public readings, special issues of scholarly journals, and symposia. Among these tributes was a thought-provoking essay by Antonio Muñoz Molina, a member of the Royal Spanish Academy known for his contributions to contemporary Spanish literature. His essay delved into the captivating themes of identity and transformation in Miguel de Cervantes' timeless masterpiece. This précis examines and elucidates Muñoz Molina's (2015) central thesis, types of evidence used, and method of argument, and highlights potential areas of debate over its interpretation of Don Quixote's identity.

© The Author(s), under exclusive license to Springer Nature Singapore Pte Ltd. 2025
O. Serrat, *Myth, Philosophy, and Literature*,
https://doi.org/10.1007/978-981-95-2897-4_9

9.2   Antonio Muñoz Molina's (2015) Insightful Tribute

"There are two kinds of people, wrote Saul Bellow in *Henderson the Rain King*: the 'be-ers' and the 'becomers.' According to Bellow, the be-ers are those who try their best to remain forever the way they are, who are content with their lives, with their names, with the places where they live. Becomers always feel ill at ease with the world as it is, and what they love are not the certainties of being, but the adventures of becoming." (Muñoz Molina 2015, p. 374). The central thesis of Muñoz Molina's (2015) essay, *Don Quixote or the Art of Becoming*, posits that the essence of *Don Quixote* (Cervantes 2003) lies in its profound exploration of identity and the process of becoming. Muñoz Molina (2015) argues that Don Quixote, the protagonist, is the first modern fictional hero because he embodies continuous self-discovery and transformation, unlike traditional epic heroes with predetermined destinies, such as Achilles or Ulysses, who remain unchanged throughout their journeys. Muñoz Molina's (2015) fascination with self-discovery and transformation is evident as he stresses that identity is not fixed but continuously shaped by choices and experiences. He references the concept of "becoming" versus "being" in literature, particularly in novels, and credits Bellow (1959) for distinguishing between "be-ers" (those content with their current state) and "becomers" (those who seek change and adventure). Muñoz Molina (2015) suggests that modern heroes are often dissatisfied with their given identities and seek to transform themselves, reflecting a broader twentieth-century ambition. Don Quixote's identity is not fixed; he actively shapes and reshapes it through his actions and imagination. This shift from a static to a dynamic conception of the hero, according to Muñoz Molina (2015), marks a significant departure from classical literature and aligns with the modern novel's focus on character development and personal growth.

9.3   The Art of Becoming in *Don Quixote*: Evidence and Method of Argument

Muñoz Molina (2015) supports his arguments with various types of evidence. He references well-known literary works and characters and includes quotes from Bellow (1959) and a speech by Robert F. Kennedy—"Some men see things as they are, and ask why. I dream of things that never were, and ask why not."—to point out the contrast between those who are content with their state and those who seek change. Additionally, Muñoz Molina (2015) provides cultural and historical context about second-generation Americans in the 1920s and 1930s, emphasizing their identity struggles and the concept of "becomers." Personal anecdotes about Bellow's childhood as an obsessive reader and Cervantes' love for written words illustrate how reading and fiction influence personal identity. Furthermore, Muñoz Molina (2015) discusses the impact of the printing press on book availability and the rise of private reading, supporting the argument that solitary reading and novels are pivotal to modern literature. He cites Spitzer's (1967) essay to provide scholarly support. By comparing the experiences of other fictional characters such as Huckleberry Finn and Holly Golightly, Muñoz Molina (2015) illustrates the theme of escaping personal identity and seeking new experiences. These pieces of evidence collectively build a compelling argument about the nature of "becoming" in literature and the distinction between "be-ers" and "becomers."

Muñoz Molina's (2015) argument is multifaceted, combining close reading, historical evidence, and theoretical perspectives. By referencing Spitzer (1967), he situates *Don Quixote* (Cervantes 2003) within a broader cultural and technological framework, discussing historical contexts such as the impact of the printing press and the rise of private reading. These developments facilitated the exploration of new ideas and identities while requiring readers to navigate the complexities of fiction and reality. This context elucidates the environment in which *Don Quixote* (Cervantes 2003) was written and its revolutionary impact.

Moreover, Muñoz Molina (2015) explores the theme of personal identity as a prison from which Don Quixote seeks to escape. Don Quixote's obsession with chivalric novels leads him to mistake fiction for reality, demonstrating the powerful impact of written words on personal identity and actions. His quest to become a knight-errant represents an attempt to break free from the constraints of his mundane life and embrace a new identity. Reading and fiction thus provide a means of escape and a way to explore new identities and possibilities.

In addition to analyzing *Don Quixote* (Cervantes 2003) and *Henderson the Rain King* (Bellow 1959), Muñoz Molina (2015) examines Tennessee Williams's *The Glass Menagerie* (2009) to firmly establish the concepts of "be-ers" and "becomers." He identifies Tom Wingfield, the central character, as a quixotic figure. Tom feeds his imagination with reading that makes him restless. His nightly excursions to the movies provide him with the strength he needs to break free from the constraints of his mundane reality, ultimately leading him to leave his job, his family, and his city. In Muñoz Molina's analysis (2015), Don Quixote is similarly portrayed as a "becomer," always striving for something beyond his current reality.

There is no doubt that Cervantes' (2003) work marked a pivotal moment in the evolution of the novel, setting the stage for the exploration of identity, transformation, and self-discovery that defines modern fiction. Hence, Muñoz Molina's (2015) well-researched thesis about Don Quixote's alignment with the "becomer" archetype is compelling. Muñoz Molina's (2015) essay is structured thematically, with each section addressing different aspects of identity and transformation. His use of rhetorical strategies, such as appeals to ethos through historical anecdotes, enhances the credibility of the argument and engages the reader.

Overall, Muñoz Molina's (2015) essay is a valuable contribution to the field of literary studies. It complements, extends, and enriches scholarly readings of *Don Quixote* (Cervantes 2003) that typically focus on character analysis, cultural and historical context, literary significance, parody and satire, or themes, offering a unique interpretation and raising important questions about identity and transformation.

9.4   Debating Muñoz Molina's Take on *Don Quixote*

However, Muñoz Molina's (2015) analysis sometimes lacks depth and gives little consideration to the other characters in *Don Quixote* (Cervantes 2003), all of whom, while secondary to the knight-errant, play crucial roles in the narrative's development and the protagonist's journey. Characters such as Sancho Panza, Dulcinea del Toboso, and the priest are not mere background figures; they provide essential counterpoints to Don Quixote's idealism and contribute immeasurably to the thematic richness of the novel. By neglecting these characters, Muñoz Molina's (2015) quixote-centric analysis risks oversimplifying the complex interplay of perspectives that Cervantes masterfully weaves into the narrative.

Muñoz Molina's (2015) quixote-centric analysis gives pride of place to the Knight of the Sorrowful Face in the exploration of the essay's thesis. In the same vein, Muñoz Molina (2015) contrasts Don Quixote with epic heroes, who remain static and unchanging. Some readers might contest this comparison, arguing that even characters such as Achilles or Ulysses, and certainly Gilgamesh—the prototypical epic hero—undergo changes and developments (Serrat 2023). For instance, Achilles' wrath and eventual reconciliation in *The Iliad* or Ulysses' journey of self-discovery in *The Odyssey* reflect remarkable character evolution.

Paradoxically, some readers might disagree with Muñoz Molina's (2015) interpretation of Don Quixote as a symbol of "becoming" rather than "being," positing that the character possesses a more stable core identity. In opposition to Muñoz Molina's (2015) thesis, they might argue that Don Quixote's actions are more about fulfilling a predetermined destiny than evolving as a character. This perspective suggests that Don Quixote's unwavering commitment to his ideals, despite the absurdity of his quests, underscores a consistent and unchanging innermost self.

Relatedly, Muñoz Molina's (2015) essay suggests that modern readers demand characters who evolve and change, unlike the static characters of earlier, pre-late-nineteenth-century literature. However, many readers might argue that there is still a place for static characters in modern literature, and that they can be just as compelling as dynamic ones. For example, archetypal characters such as James Bond, Sherlock Holmes, or Hercule Poirot remain largely unchanged across their stories, yet they continue to captivate audiences with their consistency and reliability.

Furthermore, alternative perspectives could suggest that Cervantes (2003) intended a more satirical critique of societal norms than a purely existential exploration of the leading role. The absurdity of Don Quixote's adventures and the reactions of those around him can be seen as a commentary on both the rigid social structures of the *Siglo de Oro* and the folly of blind adherence to outdated ideals.

Taken as a whole, Muñoz Molina's (2015) essay is deeply rooted in a specific cultural and literary context within broader literary themes, such as existentialism and postmodernism. For that reason, readers from different backgrounds might have different interpretations of *Don Quixote* (Cervantes 2003) and might not fully agree with Muñoz Molina's (2015) perspective. To situate Muñoz Molina's (2015) essay within the wider academic discourse, it would be useful to reference other scholarly works that contradict or support his thesis. A comparative analysis with other interpretations of *Don Quixote* (Cervantes 2003) would undoubtedly facilitate a better evaluation and appreciation of the contributions of Muñoz Molina's (2015) essay.

References

Bellow S (1959) Henderson the rain king. Viking Press

Cervantes Miguel de (2003) Don Quixote (trans: Grossman E). HarperCollins. (Original work published 1605 and 1615)

Muñoz Molina A (2015) Don Quixote or the art of becoming. Hudson Rev. 68(3):373–382. https://hudsonreview.com/2015/10/don-quixote-or-the-art-of-becoming/

Serrat O (2023). Gilgamesh: an epic for all seasons. Unpublished manuscript, Georgetown University. https://www.researchgate.net/publication/376758284_Gilgamesh_An_Epic_for_All_Seasons

Spitzer L (1967) Linguistic perspectivism in Don Quixote. In: Linguistics and literary history. Princeton University Press, p 41–86

Williams T (2009) The glass menagerie. Penguin Classics. (Original work published 1945)

10

From *Don Quixote* to Post-Truth: Baroque Insights for Modern Times

10.1 Re: The Post-Truth Phenomenon

It is proof of literature's enduring relevance that Castillo and Egginton (2022) discovered in *Don Quixote* (Cervantes, 1605/1615/2003), a groundbreaking novel penned in two parts over 400 years ago, insights that bridge the centuries and help navigate our contemporary, truth-optional world. Today, a complex web of factors—such as confirmation bias, economic incentives to spread disinformation, erosion of trust, information overload, lack of critical thinking, misinformation, political polarization, propaganda, and the influence of social media—contributes to the rise of conspiracy theories and denialism (Serrat 2014). These elements challenge public truth claims and fundamentally alter how public opinion is shaped. Consequently, in our post-truth era, objective facts often take a backseat to emotional appeals, personal beliefs, and sensational narratives, impairing rational discourse, especially in politics. This shift underscores the importance of critically examining the sources and motivations behind the information we consume—a cautionary lesson that Cervantes (1605/1615/2003) remarkably foresaw.

© The Author(s), under exclusive license to Springer Nature Singapore Pte Ltd. 2025
O. Serrat, *Myth, Philosophy, and Literature*,
https://doi.org/10.1007/978-981-95-2897-4_10

10.2 Reality Literacy and the Humanities: Lessons From *Don Quixote*

In their book, *What Would Cervantes Do? Navigating Post-Truth with Spanish Baroque Literature*, Castillo and Egginton (2022) suggested that the humanities can help resist the commodification of information in the "market society" (p. 9), a term coined by Sandel (2012). To that end, Castillo and Egginton (2022) championed "reality literacy" (p. 17)—the art of interpreting and comprehending reality—a notion originally introduced by Cervantes (1605/1615/2003). "Cervantes looks to madness as an analytical instrument," Castillo and Egginton (2022, p. 121) explained to advance their concept. In brief, *Don Quixote* (Cervantes, 1605/1615/2003) chronicled the picaresque adventures of a lucid madman (or misguided sage) in 17th-century Spain, whom Castillo and Egginton (2022) characterized as a "tangential clairvoyant" (p. 128). As a result of his excessive reading of chivalric romances, Don Quixote, the protagonist, becomes obsessed with tales of knights, heroic quests, and noble deeds. He sets out to revive knighthood and often blames an enchanter for his misfortunes. Don Quixote's absurd quest explores the blurred lines between reality and illusion by opening "oblique views [...] that reveal the nonsense of comfortable narratives and commonplace notions" (Castillo and Egginton 2022, p. 121). In the prologue to *Don Quixote*, Cervantes (1605/1615/2003) encourages readers to scrutinize the narratives they encounter: he humorously discusses his own struggles with writing the introduction and the book itself and, by presenting himself as an unreliable narrator, challenges the notion that history is purely objective and that fiction is purely subjective.

In relation to the "fake news" phenomenon, Castillo and Egginton (2022) explored the parallels between the fragility of facts in contemporary times and the general foreboding at the close of Spain's Golden Age (1492–1659), when Cervantes was writing. At the end of an era marked by outstanding artistic and cultural achievements, Spain's fast-growing readership was grappling with the nation's declining influence and worsening domestic poverty (France, 2022). During the *Siglo de Oro*, chivalric, picaresque, pastoral, and religious literature, along with drama, novellas, and poetry, captivated the literary scene. Cervantes's critique of literature in *Don Quixote* was ahead of its time. By satirizing the chivalric romances and picaresque tales popular during that period, he highlighted the potential dangers of literature that distorts reality and promotes unrealistic ideals. This likely explains the novel's universality and enduring popularity in the 21st century, perhaps even more so than in the 20th century. This suggests that writers have a significant responsibility to their readers, emphasizing the importance of truth and authenticity in storytelling. Cervantes used humor and irony to expose the absurdities of exaggerated tales, depicting how they can lead individuals to lose touch with reality. "In other words, Cervantes was both touting the value of ideal and calling attention to our failure to realize it in the present" (Castillo and Egginton 2022, p. 133; Serrat 2024a). Cervantes's critique remains relevant today, as it reminds us to be wary of the media we consume and to seek out narratives that reflect genuine human experiences.

Don Quixote (Cervantes, 1605/1615/2003) is an inspirational and poignant reflection on how subjective realities can overshadow objective truth. In my view, as we delve into the novel, five timeless insights from Cervantes stand out, each resonating even 400 years later in our reality-agnostic setting: (i) narratives shape our worldview, (ii) perception often clashes with reality, (iii) truth is multifaceted and open to interpretation, (iv) idealism counters cynicism and upholds noble values, and (v) an unwavering spirit helps us navigate contested realities.

In the musical titled *Man of La Mancha*, Wasserman (1966) had Cervantes exclaim: "When life itself seems lunatic, who knows where madness lies? Too much sanity may be madness. To seek treasure where there is only trash. Perhaps to be practical is madness. And maddest of all, to see life as it is and not as it ought to be" (p. 64). Wasserman (1966) embraced Cervantes's assertion that fiction can craft a reality more vivid and compelling than the real world: his words are so authentically Cervantine that they might have been spoken by The Knight of the Sorrowful Countenance himself.

10.3 Postscript

An interesting note: In 1637, Descartes addressed the epistemological challenge of solipsism, aiming to establish a foundation for certain knowledge beyond the self (Descartes 2004; Serrat 2024b). Intriguingly, based on the dates of the first French translation of *Don Quixote* (1614 and 1618) and the similarities between the *malin génie* (evil genius or demon) in Descartes' philosophical work and Don Quixote's enchanter, Egginton (2012) suggested that the novel played a role in shaping the foundations of modern philosophy.

References

Castillo D, Egginton W (2022) What would Cervantes do? Navigating post-truth with Spanish Baroque literature. McGill-Queen's University Press

Cervantes M de (2003) Don Quixote. (trans: Grossman E). (Original work published 1605/1615) HarperCollins

Descartes R (2004) A discourse on method: Meditations and principles. (trans: Veitch J) (Original work published 1637) Orion Publishing Group

Egginton W (2012, November 19). The novel and the origins of modern philosophy. Arcade. https://shc.stanford.edu/arcade/interventions/novel-and-origins-modern-philosophy

France M (2022, June 24). Choosing your reality: advice from the golden age of Spanish literature. Times literary supplement. https://www.the-tls.co.uk/literature/literary-criticism/what-would-cervantes-do-david-r-castillo-william-egginton-book-review-miranda-france

Sandel M (2012) What money can't buy: The moral limits of markets. Farrar, Straus and Giroux

Serrat O (2014). Information overload in the attention economy [Powerpoint slides]. https://www.researchgate.net/publication/275155424_Information_Overload_in_the_Attention_Economy

Serrat O (2024a). Exploring identity: Antonio Muñoz Molina's (2015) take on Don Quixote. Unpublished manuscript, Georgetown University, https://www.researchgate.net/publication/385290348_Exploring_Identity_Antonio_Munoz_Molina's_2015_Take_on_Don_Quixote

Serrat O (2024b). Knowing that and knowing how: must it be either/or? Unpublished manuscript, Georgetown University, https://www.researchgate.net/publication/379514661_Knowing_That_and_Knowing_How_Must_It_Be_EitherOr

Wasserman D (1966) Man of La Mancha. Prompt Book

11

From Page to Screen: Adapting *Don Quixote* for a New Era

11.1 Reimagining a Classic: Gilliam's Cinematic Odyssey

Terry Gilliam's (2018) *The Man Who Killed Don Quixote* is a cinematic odyssey that reimagines Cervantes's (1605/1615/2003) timeless tale for a contemporary audience. This adaptation follows Toby Grummett, a jaded and cynical film director, trapped in the delusions of an old Spanish cobbler who takes himself for Don Quixote. Mistaken for Sancho Panza, Toby is pulled into surreal and comic adventures and forced to confront the consequences of a film he made in his youth, which had a profound impact on the cobbler. The performances of Adam Driver (Toby Grummett/"Sancho Panza") and Jonathan Pryce (Javier Sanchez/ "Don Quixote") have been praised for their depth and humor. This précis examines how Gilliam's (2018) film not only adapts but also, to a lesser extent, appropriates the original text. By seamlessly blending fantasy and reality, the film crafts a narrative rich in cultural commentary, complex characters, current themes, and a distinctive visual style that deeply resonates with today's viewers. Ultimately, Gilliam's (2018) film serves as both a tribute to and a transformation of Cervantes's (1605/1615/ 2003) masterpiece, demonstrating the enduring relevance of classic literature in contemporary cinema.

O. Serrat, *Myth, Philosophy, and Literature*,
https://doi.org/10.1007/978-981-95-2897-4_11

11.2 Faithful Adaptation or Radical Reworking?

Adaptation generally seeks to remain faithful to the source material, but appropriation is a more radical reworking that often serves a new political or social purpose (Sanders 2016). In her book, *Adaptation and Appropriation*, Julie Sanders (2016) explores the complex and varied nature of the two processes. She explains that adaptation involves transforming an existing text into a new form—such as a film, a novel, or a play—while typically retaining the core elements (i.e., plot, characters, themes). She examines the aesthetic and cultural politics that motivate adaptations, showing how they can reflect and respond to different cultural contexts, mediums, and theoretical movements. This exploration underscores the importance of adaptation as a dynamic process that both re-explains original works and engages with modern cultural and theoretical discourses. Conversely, Sanders (2016) explains that appropriation aims to critique the original work, modifying the source material to challenge its original context or meanings and to create something that reflects present-day issues or perspectives.

11.3 The Arduous Process of Adaptation

Gilliam's (2018) *The Man Who Killed Don Quixote* is a testament to the arduous process of adaptation, especially when it intertwines with a creator's vision and the vicissitudes of film production. The film's narrative mirrors the quixotic pursuit of the ideal adaptation itself. The making of the film was fraught with difficulties, including legal disputes and production setbacks, which reflect the broader complexities involved in adapting a canonical text such as *Don Quixote* (Cervantes, 1605/1615/2003) for contemporary audiences. The film becomes a meta-commentary not only on the original work but also on the nature of storytelling and the boundaries of adaptation.

11.4 Divergence and Resonance: A Contemporary Lens

Critics might argue that Gilliam's (2018) adaptation diverges too significantly from Cervantes's (1605/1615/2003) original narrative, conceivably alienating purists who value fidelity to the source material. However, this divergence is precisely what allows the film to resonate with current viewers, as it reimagines the classic tale through a present-day lens. For example, Gilliam's (2018) version distributes qualities of the knight and his squire across multiple characters, complicating the traditional Don Quixote/Sancho dynamic and enriching the narrative with a broader spectrum of perspectives. The character of the "real" Sancho Panza, for instance, makes a brief appearance in the film, a significant departure from the novel where he is a constant companion to Don Quixote. This alteration allows the film to delve into the psyche of its protagonist, Toby, who embodies both the idealism of Don Quixote and the pragmatism of Sancho Panza.

11.5 Whimsy and Reality: Gilliam's Signature Visual Style

Another potential counterargument is that the film's whimsical and surreal visual style might overshadow the narrative's depth. However, Gilliam's signature visual style grounds the fantastical elements of *Don Quixote* (Cervantes, 1605/1615/2003) in a recognizable actuality. The result is a film that feels both familiar and innovative, paying homage to the spirit of the original work while boldly reimagining it for a new generation. The female characters in Gilliam's (2018) film, for example, are given more agency than in the original text. Dulcinea is transformed into a character with her own narrative and creative power, redefining the passive role assigned in the novel. This change not only updates the story for today's viewers but also reflects the evolving roles of women in society and storytelling.

11.6 The Quixotic Pursuit of an Impossible Dream

The film's production history mirrors the themes of adaptation and perseverance. After numerous setbacks over nearly three decades, Gilliam's (2018) vision for *The Man Who Killed Don Quixote* finally came to fruition, embodying the quixotic pursuit of an impossible dream. This metanarrative adds another layer to the film's exploration of adaptation, as the process of bringing the story to the screen becomes a reflection of some of the novel's core themes, such as idealism and pragmatism, madness and sanity, and the blurred lines between illusion and reality.

11.7 Understanding Gilliam's Approach Through Sanders's Lens

Sanders's (2016) framework helps us understand Gilliam's (2018) approach. Yes, Gilliam (2018) adapts the form of *Don Quixote* (Cervantes, 1605/1615/ 2003) to suit a contemporary narrative, but he also appropriates its thematic essence. The result is a hybrid that honors the spirit of the original through a transformative lens, engaging with the cultural and aesthetic politics behind the impulse to adapt as outlined by Sanders (2016). Gilliam's (2018) film, much like Sanders's (2016) description of appropriation, becomes a complex negotiation of style and meaning, where the original text is not just adapted but is reimagined and imbued with new relevance.

11.8 A Complex Tapestry of Adaptation

Terry Gilliam's 2018 film, *The Man Who Killed Don Quixote*, is a rich tapestry of adaptation, seamlessly blending elements of the original novel with contemporary interpretations and modern-day anxieties (Serrat 2024). Through significant changes in character dynamics, narrative focus, and thematic exploration, Gilliam (2018) creates a film that is both a tribute to and a transformation of Cervantes's (1605/1615/2003) masterpiece, demonstrating the creative potential of adaptation and showing that even the most well-known stories can be retold in fresh and meaningful ways.

References

Cervantes M de (2003) Don Quixote. (trans: Grossman E,). HarperCollins. (Original work published 1605/1615)

Gilliam T, Grisoni T. (Writers), Gilliam T. (Director). (2018). The man who killed Don Quixote [Film]. Alacran Pictures; Tornasol Films; Kinology; Entre Chien et Loup; Ukbar Filmes; El Hombre Que Mato a Don Quijote AIE; Carisco Producciones AIE; Recorded Picture Company

Sanders J (2016) Adaptation and appropriation, 2nd edn. Routledge

Serrat O (2024). From Don Quixote to post-truth: Baroque insights for modern times. Unpublished manuscript, Georgetown University. https://www.research gate.net/publication/385740067_From_Don_Quixote_to_Post-Truth_ Baroque_Insights_for_Modern_Times

12

Reading Through Time: Navigating Change with Literary Theory

12.1 Literary Theory: A Pillar of Intellectual Inquiry

Rita Felski navigated a complex terrain in her reproof of the "knowingness" of literary criticism (Felski 2008, p. 4): she simultaneously promoted a "hybrid phenomenology" (Felski 2008, p. 17) and "postcritical reading," a new theory in literary studies "not to be confused with the uncritical" (Felski 2015, p. 173; Serrat 2024). A self-declared feminist theorist (Felski 2008, p. 9), Felski was not about to refute scholarly interpretation of written works.

Literature with a capital L—typically defined as work of lasting artistic or cultural merit—explores and expresses human experience: it encompasses a wide range of themes and subjects that reflect life's manifold complexities. Literary theory, in turn, provides analytical frameworks to help us understand, interpret, and critique literary texts. Far from being a collection of abstract concepts, literary theory emerges in communities of readers and writers through critical thinking and philosophical inquiry about, say, cultural, economic, environmental, political, and social contexts (Culler 2011). Despite Felski's (Felski 2008, 2015) censure, theoretical reflection is here to stay: it will continue to be a vital part of our intellectual milieu, evolving and uncovering new meanings by way of context, intention, reader, and text (Culler 2011). This process will not be limited to literature but will extend to film and digital content, making these media accessible and relevant to contemporary audiences.

© The Author(s), under exclusive license to Springer Nature Singapore Pte Ltd. 2025
O. Serrat, *Myth, Philosophy, and Literature*,
https://doi.org/10.1007/978-981-95-2897-4_12

Felski (2008) aimed to carve out a niche with her focus on postcritical reading. In contrast, Klages (2017) sought to integrate schools of thought and offer a comprehensive overview rather than concentrate on a singular theoretical approach. Klages (2017) discoursed on the major schools of literary theory, including deconstruction, ecocriticism, feminist theories, ideology and discourse, postmodernism, psychoanalysis, queer theories, race and postcolonialism, and structuralism.

12.2 Contextualizing Literary Theory: The Importance of Historical Circumstances

Klages (2017) purported to provide a "complete" guide to literary theory but could have underscored the historical circumstances that have shaped it, including the impact of major events (e.g., social movements, technological advancements, wars). Literary theory is dynamic, and a portrayal of how theories adapt over time would offer richer understanding. Furthermore, Klages (2017) might have delved into the intersections of literary theory with other disciplines (e.g., philosophy, political science, sociology), and how these intersections have evolved historically. Moreover, Klages's (2017) work emphasized Western literary theory and gave comparatively little attention to non-Western perspectives such as those from African, Arabic, Chinese, Indian, Japanese traditions.

12.3 Enter Posthumanism

A recent literary theory not mentioned in Klages (2017) is posthumanism. Born of remarkable technological advancements in recent decades, posthumanism examines the boundaries between humans, technology (e.g., artificial intelligence, biotechnology, cybernetics, genetic engineering, life extension, nanotechnology, neural interfaces, augmented reality, virtual reality), and the environment (Braidotti 2013; Ferrando 2019; Hayles 1999; Wolfe 2009). Posthumanism challenges traditional notions of human identity and agency with key concepts that include:

- **Cyborg Theory.** This concept explores the blurring lines between humans and machines, suggesting that humans are already cyborgs due to their reliance on technology and positing that this integration will deepen (Haraway 1991).

- **Decentering the Human.** This concept challenges the traditional human-centric view of the world, emphasizing the interconnectedness of all forms of life and technology.
- **Post-Anthropocentrism.** This concept views humans as one species within an interconnected web of multispecies living on Earth, inviting us to consider the agency and value of non-human entities.
- **Transhumanism.** This concept advocates the use of technology to enhance the cognitive and physical abilities of humans.

Posthumanism has applications and implications across various domains: prominent among these are ethics and identity, as posthumanism raises profound questions about the ethical treatment of non-human entities and the essence of being human. Posthumanism also examines the societal impact of emerging technologies, such as genetic modifications, health implications, infodemics, misinformation, privacy, and surveillance. Additionally, posthumanism intersects with ecocriticism, offering visions for the future that include sustainable living and technological integration. As technologies continue to evolve and the boundaries between humans and machines blur, posthumanism will likely gain traction, prompting us to reconsider our relationship with the planet and each other.

12.4 Literary Theory: A Vital Compass for Ever-Changing Landscapes

Literary theory serves as a vital compass with which to navigate the ever-changing landscape of literature, guiding readers through the complexities of textual interpretation and cultural context. By embracing diverse theoretical perspectives, we not only deepen our understanding of literary works but also enrich our appreciation of the dynamic interplay between literature and society. As we read through time, literary theory empowers us to engage with change thoughtfully, ensuring that literature's transformative power remains a beacon for future generations.

References

Braidotti R (2013) The posthuman. Polity

Culler J (2011) Literary theory: a very short introduction. 2nd edn. Oxford University Press

Felski R (2008) Uses of literature. Blackwell Publishing

Felski R (2015) The limits of critique. University of Chicago Press

Ferrando F (2019) Philosophical posthumanism. Bloomsbury Academic

Haraway D (1991) Simians, cyborgs, and women: the reinvention of nature. Routledge

Hayles N (1999) How we became posthuman: virtual bodies in cybernetics, literature, and informatics. University of Chicago Press

Klages M (2017) Literary theory: the complete guide. Bloomsbury Publishing

Serrat O (2024). Recognition, enchantment, knowledge, and shock: a response to Felski's literary phenomenology. Unpublished manuscript, Georgetown University. https://www.researchgate.net/publication/384079872_Recognition_Enchantment_Knowledge_and_Shock_A_Response_to_Felski's_2008_Literary_Phenomenology

Wolfe C (2009) What is posthumanism? University of Minnesota Press

13

Recognition, Enchantment, Knowledge, and Shock: A Response to Felski's (2008) Literary Phenomenology

13.1 *Uses of Literature* (Felski, 2008): An Un-Manifesto

"What follows is [...] an un-manifesto: a negation of a negation, an act of yea-saying not nay-saying, a thought experiment that seeks to advocate, not denigrate," Felski (2008, p. 1) declared in the introduction to her book. An unconventional manifesto Felski (2008) certainly was: *Uses of Literature* challenged the "knowingness" of ideological criticism, which, far from being synonymous with "knowing," Felski (2008) understood as "a stance of permanent skepticism and sharply honed suspicion" (p. 4). Running counter to prevailing currents of literary theory, namely, "the systematic account of the nature of literature and of the methods for analyzing it" (Culler 2011, p. 1), Felski (2008) aimed to rediscover reasons for reading, no less.

13.2 The Frankfurt School: Pioneers of Critical Theory

Inspired by Sigmund Freud, Karl Marx, and Friedrich Nietzsche among others, an illustrious group of cultural critics, philosophers, and sociologists counting Theodor Adorno, Walter Benjamin, Erich Fromm, Max Horkheimer, and Herbert Marcuse had resolved in the 1920s to expose and challenge the power structures that condition society according to class, gender, race, and other differences. Contrary to the traditional view that theory

© The Author(s), under exclusive license to Springer Nature Singapore Pte Ltd. 2025
O. Serrat, *Myth, Philosophy, and Literature*,
https://doi.org/10.1007/978-981-95-2897-4_13

governs the sciences, the so-called Frankfurt School asserted that theory is historical, subjective, and part of society (Buchanan 2018). Critical theory had a profound impact on social sciences and humanities (e.g., community psychology, cultural studies, education, history, law, philosophy, political science, sociology), reshaping how scholars and practitioners approach their fields: it also influenced literary theory through new methodologies including critical discourse analysis, deconstruction, ecocriticism, feminist theories, postmodernism, queer theories, race and postcolonial studies, and structuralism, which over the period 1950–1990 transformed the analysis and interpretation of texts (Klages 2017). "Critical reading" became the chief object of literary studies: to Felski's (2008) chagrin, all value was in academia assigned to the act of reading and none to the works read (pp. 2–3).

13.3 Celebrating Everyday Reading: Felski's Affective Turn

Moved by what is lost when literature is subjected to "permanent diagnosis," Felski (2008, p. 1) determined to celebrate everyday reading and underscore the affective dimensions of reading. Felski (2008) proposed "that reading involves a logic of *recognition*; that aesthetic experience has analogies with *enchantment* in a supposedly disenchanted age; that literature creates distinctive configurations of social *knowledge*; [and] that we may value the experience of being *shocked* by what we read" (p. 14) This is not to say that Felski (2008), a feminist theorist herself, was turning her back on scholarly interpretation: "A respect for everyday perceptions is entirely compatible with a commitment to theory," Felski (2008, p. 15) affirmed. Rather, Felski (2008) aimed with a self-avowed hybrid phenomenology "to give equal weight to cognitive and affective aspects of aesthetic response" (p. 16), to reinvigorate literary theory with the vitality of the everyday. "No more separate spheres!" Felski (2015) exclaimed in a longer monograph on the limits of critique (p. 11).

13.4 Modes of Textual Engagement: Recognition, Enchantment, Knowledge, Shock

Recognition, enchantment, knowledge, and shock, which Felski (2008) termed "modes of textual engagement" (p. 14), are different ways to think about why we read literature. Recognition is the experience of seeing oneself in a book, a process—some might detect a human need—that is both ordinary and mysterious as it involves knowing again, perhaps knowing better, something that is familiar (Felski 2008, pp. 23–50). Enchantment refers to a state of intense involvement, or willing suspension of disbelief, during which a reader is completely absorbed by the aesthetic experience of a text for a momentary escape from reality (Felski 2008, pp. 51–76). Knowledge intuits that reading serves as a valuable source of learning and reflection, providing insights into culture, human nature, and society to enrich our emotional and intellectual lives and broaden our perspectives on the world (Felski 2008, pp. 77–104) Shock relates to the ability of a text to upset a reader's expectations; by provoking a strong emotional or intellectual response, shock helps us question assumptions and encourages critical reflection to also transform our worldviews (Felski 2008, pp. 105–131).

Felski (2008) acknowledged that her "modes of textual engagement" drew from such traditional aesthetic categories as anagnorisis (recognition), beauty (enchantment), mimesis (knowledge), and the sublime (shock) (p. 15). Felski (2008) clarified that her "modes of textual engagement" are neither all-encompassing nor mutually exclusive; rather, Felski (2008) highlighted strands of aesthetic response she detected were frequently intertwined and even interfused (p. 15). But, what of such other "modes of textual engagement" as the comic, the grotesque, the pastoral, the picturesque, the tragic, or, say, the ugly (which is the opposite of beauty), one might ask? Adding other "modes of textual engagement" could enrich Felski's (2008) framework by highlighting additional dimensions of reader engagement, thereby offering a more comprehensive picture of the reading experience. Incorporating other "modes of textual engagement" in Felski's (2008) framework might dilute the clarity and focus of the original four, complicate the framework with possibly overlapping categories, and make it less focused and harder to apply consistently across different texts and reading experiences. Even so, expanding Felski's (2008) framework would open avenues for research in aesthetic theory, comparative literature, digital humanities, genre studies, interdisciplinary studies, pedagogical approaches, and reader-response theory.

13.5 Beyond the Hermeneutics of Suspicion

Transcending the limits of traditional critique that aims to unmask and demystify literary works, Felski's (2008) book offers a fruitful exploration of the diverse roles that literature plays in our lives, encouraging readers to engage with texts in meaningful ways. Comprising four succinct yet comprehensive chapters, enriched with examples from a broad spectrum of national literary traditions, Felski's (2008) work is a refreshing contribution in a field often dominated, following Paul Ricœur, by the "hermeneutics of suspicion" (p. 34).

References

Buchanan I (2018) Oxford dictionary of critical theory. 2nd edn. Oxford University Press

Culler J (2011) Literary theory: a very short introduction. 2nd edn. Oxford University Press

Felski R (2008) Uses of literature. Blackwell Publishing

Felski R (2015) The limits of critique. University of Chicago Press

Klages M (2017) Literary theory: the complete guide. Bloomsbury Publishing

Index

Zeitfracht Medien GmbH
Ferdinand-Jühlke-Straße 7
99095 Erfurt, Deutschland
produktsicherheit@kolibri360.de